Buzz to Brilliance

Buzz to Brilliance

A Beginning and Intermediate
Guide to Trumpet Playing

Adrian D. Griffin

with Elise Winters-Huete

OXFORD
UNIVERSITY PRESS

Oxford University Press is a department of the University of Oxford. It furthers the University's objective of
excellence in research, scholarship, and education by publishing worldwide.

Oxford   New York
Auckland   Cape Town   Dar es Salaam   Hong Kong   Karachi
Kuala Lumpur   Madrid   Melbourne   Mexico City   Nairobi
New Delhi   Shanghai   Taipei   Toronto

With offices in
Argentina   Austria   Brazil   Chile   Czech Republic   France   Greece
Guatemala   Hungary   Italy   Japan   Poland   Portugal   Singapore
South Korea   Switzerland   Thailand   Turkey   Ukraine   Vietnam

Oxford is a registered trade mark of Oxford University Press in the UK and certain other countries.

Published in the United States of America by
Oxford University Press
198 Madison Avenue, New York, NY 10016

Library of Congress Cataloging-in-Publication Data
Griffin, Adrian D., 1975–
Buzz to brilliance : a beginning and intermediate guide to trumpet playing /
by Adrian D. Griffin, with Elise Winters.
p. cm.
Includes index.
ISBN 978-0-19-539597-6; 978-0-19-539598-3 (pbk.)
1. Trumpet — Instruction and study. I. Winters, Elise. II. Title.
MT440.G75 2012
788.9'2193 — dc22 2009042481

ISBN 978-0-19-539597-6; 978-0-19-539598-3 (pbk.)

1 3 5 7 9 8 6 4 2

Printed in the United States of America on acid-free paper

Prescription Drug Precaution:

The information in the book does not replace a doctor's guidance and the drug information that accompanies medication.
Performers for whom performance anxiety is a significant hindrance to their playing should consult a psychiatrist about
whether their anxiety is problematic and merits a prescription for an anxiety-reducing medication. Meditation, relaxation
exercises, and cognitive behavioral therapy offer the best first-line approach to dealing with performance anxiety.

A graduate of the Cincinnati-Conservatory of Music, Adrian D. Griffin has toured the United States and Mexico as a trumpet soloist, clinician, and performer.

A finalist for the International Trumpet Guild Solo Competition at the age of 23, Adrian has performed with the Louisville Orchestra, Kentucky Symphony, Lexington Philharmonic, Moscow Radio Symphony, Conspirare, Victoria Bach Festival, Austin Symphony, Austin Lyric Opera, and the Virginia Symphony Orchestra.

Adrian has held positions including the co-principal trumpet with the Orquesta Sinfónica de Monterrey, Ballet de Monterrey, and Opera Metropolitana de Monterrey; fourth trumpet with the Virginia Symphony Orchestra; and trumpet professor at the University of Texas at San Antonio. He is currently principal trumpet with the Filarmónica de Jalisco in Guadalajara, Mexico.

A signed artist and clinician for Conn/Selmer and Bach Trumpets, Adrian is the first person in North America to be a Denis

Wick featured artist. He has presented master classes and clinics throughout Mexico and North America, including the prestigious Texas Bandmasters Convention.

Adrian has published numerous articles in *Instrumentalist Magazine*. Adrian completed *Buzz to Brilliance* after nearly a decade of research and writing. For more information, visit www.adriangriffin.com.

A member of the Austin Symphony Orchestra for twelve years, Elise Winters began studying violin at the age of four and was a finalist in the National Symphony Young Artists Competition at the age of sixteen. She performs with the Austin Chamber Music Center, Chamber Soloists of Austin, Salon Concerts, Conspirare, and the Austin Lyric Opera. A graduate *summa cum laude* of Rice University and the University of Texas, she is currently authoring a violin method book which synthesizes the best elements of Suzuki, Kodály, and folk traditions.

Preface for Students

Welcome to *Buzz to Brilliance*, and congratulations on choosing to play the trumpet! An amazing musical voyage lies ahead of you. Your only limitations are your imagination and your discipline—your willingness to work at uncovering the music that's waiting to come out of your trumpet!

Each chapter in this book is chosen specifically for you, to give you everything you need during your first several years of playing the trumpet. Beyond the basics you need to start playing, you will find topics such as trumpet history, cleaning your trumpet, dealing with frustration, auditioning, and much, much more.

You will notice that some topics (for example, instrument care and practicing) are covered very thoroughly in the book, while other chapters are much more concise. In choosing the information to include in the book, my intention has been to avoid "paralysis through analysis," in which thinking too much about the skill actually interferes with your body's natural abilities. *Buzz to Brilliance* is designed to complement your musical journey in every way; to give you the information that will make a real difference for you—technically, musically, and professionally.

The exercises in the last section of *Buzz to Brilliance* span several levels of development, from beginner to advanced player. To help you more easily find material suited to your needs, the exercises are labeled as follows:

Cornerstone	These are the main building blocks to trumpet playing, designed to be practiced regularly over many years of study.	
Beginner	Intended for students in their first year of study.	
Intermediate	Perfect for the player who knows the basics and is beginning to move toward mastery.	
Advanced	Designed for the player who has mastered the fundamentals of trumpet playing, who is extending their technique and deepening their musicality.	

The various "Cornerstone" exercises are additionally marked "Beginner," "Intermediate," or "Advanced," indicating the level you should have attained when you first begin working on them.

Although *Buzz to Brilliance* is designed to be read from front to back, you may be someone who prefers to jump directly to sections you find most useful. If you do skip around, be sure to read chapters 7 and 8 before reading anything later in the book. These chapters discuss practice strategies that will keep your chops in shape! Following those suggestions will make later chapters more effective.

It was my pleasure to write this book for you, and I am honored to share your trumpet journey with you!

Preface for Teachers

This book is intended to be used as a resource for beginning to intermediate trumpet players of any age who want to improve their technique and learn more about the trumpet. It should be used in conjunction with method books such as Arban, Schlossberg, and the student's classroom text. Band teachers may recommend this book to their students to help them develop their technique and musicality and prepare for advanced study.

This book reflects my desire to pass the best of my teachers' legacies to the next generation. The ideas presented here synthesize some of the best information and teaching available, organized and explained for a younger audience.

By introducing and reinforcing crucial information outside of class time, this book offers band directors and private teachers an opportunity to spend more of their time simply sharing music with their students—the most rewarding part of teaching!

Special Acknowledgments

would like to express my appreciation to the following people who have had a direct and indirect influence on my teaching and playing, and who have contributed to this book in various ways.

First and foremost, thank you to my father, Wendell L. Griffin, my first musical role model who continues to inspire me with his own trumpet playing.

Jonathan Gresham, Marie Speziale, Steve Pride, Ray Sasaki, Jerome Amend, Michael Tunnell, Ronald Romm, Kerry Taylor, Susan Glover, Gil Lettow, Wynton Marsalis, Rodney Winther, and Gary Whitis have touched my life and my playing in many ways, and I am grateful for their musical and personal contributions. A special thank you to my mother, Belinda K. Griffin, for teaching me the patience and perseverance to complete such a project.

Thanks to Tim Shaffer for the transcriptions of the musical exercises, to David Bolton for the illustrations throughout the book, and Kris Anderson for lending his posture and embouchure for the photographs in the book. To David Hickman for his boundless expertise in all things trumpet. To John Jarger and the students of the Lake Travis High School Band for various student photos. To Conn-Selmer, Reunion Blues, Denis Wick, Schilke Trumpets, Sabine Company, and Bach Trumpets for many of the reference photos used throughout the book.

I would like to reserve a special thank-you for my co-author Elise Winters, for a remarkable four-year collaboration, culminating in a summer of e-mails between Monterrey, Mexico and Austin, Texas. Elise's diligence and attention to detail kept me constantly on my toes during the process of writing the book, and it would not have been possible without her.

Additional Sources

While innumerable texts and literature have in some way contributed to the information in this book through their impact on the trumpet pedagogy, I would like to reserve special mention for a few texts which have served as resources during the writing of the book.

Students are encouraged to refer to these texts for comprehensive explanations of many additional topics ranging from history to physics to anatomy. These books go into greater detail on various topics than was possible in these pages, and can answer many of the questions advanced players may have as they continue their study.

Invaluable information on various brass-related topics came from Scott Whitener's *A Complete Guide to Brass*, Arnold Jacobs' *Song and Wind*, Dan Bachelder and Norman Hunt's *Guide to Teaching Brass*, Rafael Mendez' *Prelude to Brass Playing*, Philip Farkas' *The Art of Brass Playing*, and David Hickman's *Trumpet Pedagogy*.

Several ongoing discussions on contentious little details were settled with the help of the *Harvard Dictionary of Music*, edited by Don Randel, and the *New Grove Dictionary of Music and Musicians*. We thank them for helping to keep the peace!

Contents

xvi

Buzz to Brilliance

1

Meet Your Trumpet

"Dinner!" my mom yelled from the kitchen.

A trumpet blared from the next room, the sound of my dad practicing for a blues band he was playing with later that night. You could hear it everywhere in our two-story house.

Between my dad's trumpet playing and the sounds of Blood Sweat and Tears, Chicago, and Chase piping from the family room next to the kitchen, our house was never quiet. Sometimes my mom pretended the music got on her nerves, but I noticed that she came to every show my dad played.

My dad was an engineer and I was just a kid, and there wasn't always much for us to talk about. Whenever he was watching a movie with good music, though, he would yell for me to run from wherever I was and watch it with him. Music was what we shared.

The summer before I started sixth grade, my dad and I were in the school gym for instrument selection night. I really wanted to play the saxophone, but my dad wanted to be able to help me practice. I was just happy to play something, so I drove home with a new trumpet sitting on my lap.

When I opened that case, I was excited. It was like the best toy I'd ever had! That changed, though, when I first put it to my lips and tried to play. No sound came out! That's when I realized this was not a toy. From that moment on, it became a challenge for me to conquer.

In those early days my dad and I would go up to my room after dinner. He would sit on my bed and show me how to clean the trumpet and play my music.

4

I loved this time with my dad. Sometimes it was hard when he criticized what I was doing, because what I wanted most in the whole world was to impress him; but I wouldn't trade that hour for anything.

A year later, I was just entering junior high. I'd been playing for a year, and was in the band room for tryouts. There was noise all around. I listened to the other players in the room, curious about how everyone played, confident that I would easily win first chair.

I heard Geoff first. In just thirty seconds it was clear where I really stood!

When I heard Seth a few minutes later, I took a deep breath and told myself that I would catch up with both of them by winter break.

The three of us were friends by the end of the first week of band, and I started practicing one or two hours every night. We spurred each other on; as soon as one of us began to surpass the others, the other two would race to catch up. Geoff, Seth, and I dominated regional and state band for the next six years.

Seth is now a fireman; Geoff is principal trumpet in the Virginia Symphony; and if my parents never know exactly what adventures we three had over the six years of band trips and other excursions, it will be a good thing.

Ready, Set . . . Wait!

Look below at the pictures of both a trumpet and a cornet (Figures 1.1 and 1.2). The instruments are basically the same, but the metal tubing is wrapped differently, and there are other subtle differences as well. Some students begin on the cornet because its more compact shape can make it easier to hold. From here on, when I say "trumpet," that also includes cornet.

If you have just purchased an instrument, there are a few things you should look for.

First, be sure that the slides and valves move easily. When you insert the mouthpiece, it should fit snugly in the leadpipe. Find the water key; the cork

FIGURE 1.1

The B♭ trumpet sets the tone for the whole band! Take out your trumpet and find the parts above. The first valve slide saddle is found on professional instruments, but is usually not included on beginning instruments.

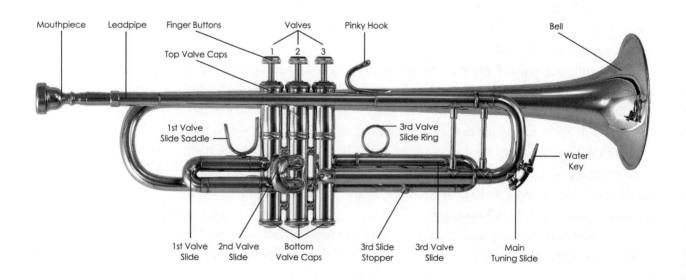

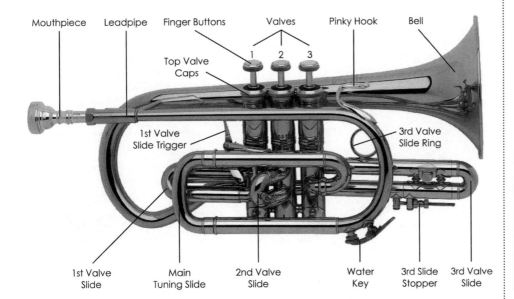

Mouthpiece Leadpipe Finger Buttons Valves Pinky Hook Bell

Top Valve Caps

1 2 3

1st Valve Slide Trigger

3rd Valve Slide Ring

1st Valve Slide Main Tuning Slide 2nd Valve Slide Water Key 3rd Slide Stopper 3rd Valve Slide

FIGURE 1.2

The cornet is wrapped slightly differently than a trumpet, and may be easier to hold for some players. Notice the first valve trigger, which may not be included on your cornet.

should be in good condition and the spring should be sturdy, making a good seal when the water key is closed.

If your instrument is used, check it for leaks, dents, and corrosion. Internal corrosion is hard to identify but may show up as tiny reddish pinpoints on the outside of the trumpet.

Finally, all trumpets are made of brass, which is then coated with either a clear acrylic or lacquer, or with silver plating. Any flaws in the plating or the lacquer should be reflected in the price of the instrument.

If possible, have your instrument tested by your music teacher or private lesson teacher to make sure the instrument is in good working order. It's not uncommon for students to have problems in the first week of practice because of faulty equipment. You have enough to concentrate on without dealing with that, too!

Respect the Brass

While they may look and sound virtually indestructible, trumpets (and cornets) are made of brass, a very soft metal that is very easy to dent and twist. Be very careful with your instrument, since even a small mishap can cause a misfit between the parts. Dings or dents will potentially cause the trumpet to play out of tune, so treat your trumpet well and keep it in its case whenever you are not actually playing.

Your slides and valves are the moving parts of your trumpet. You'll need to keep them lubricated and clean so that they move freely. Make sure you have a mouthpiece brush, snake, slide grease, and valve oil (Figure 1.3) for this purpose.

If you are buying a used instrument, make sure it is professionally cleaned before you begin practice. If you are buying from a private individual rather

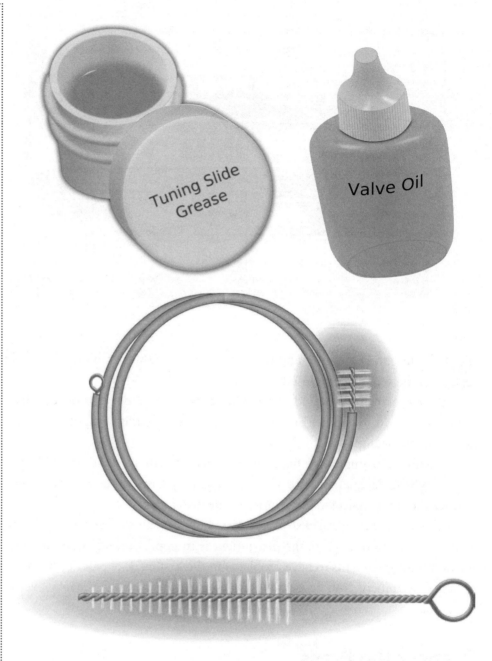

than a music store, ask them if they will adjust the price to allow for professional cleaning.

Three Valves, Twelve Notes

A valve is a mechanism that allows a pipe to be sealed or opened, increasing the length of the air column and thereby lowering the pitch (Figure 1.4). Each valve opens a corresponding tube when pressed, and can be pressed alone or in combination. Each fingering combination essentially creates a trumpet of a different length! The three valves, working with the lips and tongue height, give you each of the twelve notes in the musical scale.

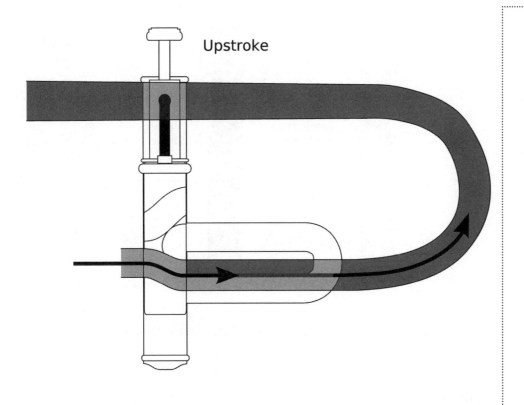

Upstroke

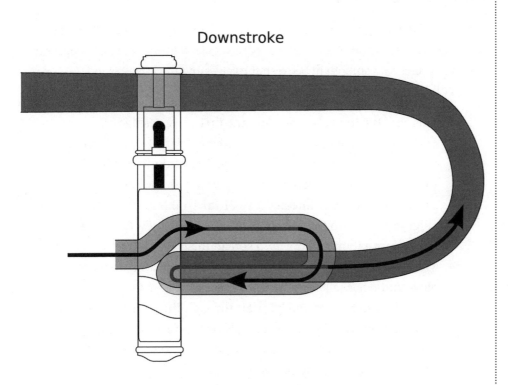

Downstroke

Each valve goes in its own section of the valve casing, and fits in one spot. The valves are designed to fit exactly, so take your time when placing them back in the casing, and never force anything. Notice that each valve has a metal or plastic valve guide, located under the valve spring. The valve guide has a jigsaw-like piece protruding on each side (Figure 1.5), which must fall into a little notch

8

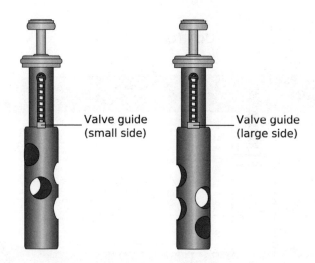

Valve guide
(small side)

Valve guide
(large side)

inside the casing and must face a particular direction to allow air to pass through the valve.

Oiling the Valves

Your valves require gentleness, respect, and occasionally some quality attention to stay in good working order. Oiling these parts regularly flushes out dirt, reduces friction, and preserves a smooth fit between the valves and the valve casing.

Follow these steps to oil your valves:

1. Unscrew the top valve cap from the first valve casing.
2. Slide the valve out of the casing until approximately an inch of the brushed silvery metal is showing. To avoid the risk of dropping the valve, leave the valve partway in the casing.
3. Place approximately fifteen drops of valve oil onto the valve (Figure 1.6). With the valve still lifted, turn it a few times, then gently move it up and down to spread the oil.
4. Then turn the valve until you hear a click, indicating that the valve guide has fallen in the right space.
5. Press the valve down and blow air through the trumpet to ensure that the valve isn't in backward. (The valve might click into place even if it's backward, but it will not allow air to pass.)
6. Screw the top valve cap onto the casing.
7. Repeat these steps for the second and third valves.
8. To circulate the oil through the valves and trumpet, press and release each valve a few times, then press all the valves down and blow air into the trumpet through the mouthpiece.
9. If you hear any gurgling in the trumpet, use the water key to empty excess oil.

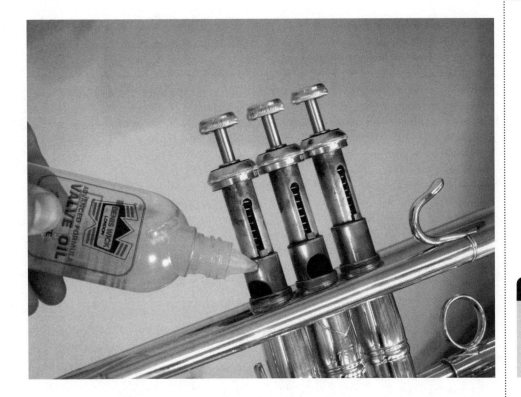

FIGURE 1.6

When oiling the valves, leave each valve in the casing to avoid the risk of dropping and damaging the valve.

Oil your valves daily for the first month after purchasing your new trumpet to minimize friction between the valves and valve casings. Wipe the valves weekly with a lint-free cloth to remove tiny metal particles caused by friction between the valves and the casing. Otherwise these particles can damage the smooth surface of the valves and valve casings. After the first month, oil your valves every other day, or as needed.

On a brand new trumpet (or cornet) the valve springs will be stiff, making your valves difficult to press. With the valves now lubricated, finger the valves using the correct right-hand position (Figure 2.4, page 20) for at least an hour to break in the springs. You can even do this while watching television. Breaking in the valves ahead of time allows for more comfort as you begin playing (the alternative is allowing the valves to break in gradually over time).

Never use spit to lubricate the valves! Besides being ineffective, the acid in your saliva will cause the metal to break down.

Slides

Using the picture of the trumpet and cornet on pages 4–5, find the three valve slides, located on the valve casing. Each of these slides is used to adjust the pitch (how high or low the note is) on that valve. To remove any of these slides, you must press the corresponding valve and keep it pressed as you remove the slide.

A Brief History of the Trumpet

The trumpet, in its many primitive forms, is one of the oldest instruments in human history, dating back several thousand years. Ancient cultures, such as those of Egypt, China, Greece, and Rome, used early ancestors of the trumpet made from shells, animal horns, and tubes of metal or wood.

In Egypt, silver and bronze trumpets more than four thousand years old were found in King Tutankhamun's tomb. Artwork from a tribal ruin in Peru offers additional evidence for the long history of the trumpet in various cultures.

In early history the trumpet was played mainly as a warning signal (because of its ability to project across great distances) and during festivities. In battle, trumpet calls served to announce troop movements, inspire the troops, and intimidate the opposing army. These early ancestors of the modern trumpet could usually produce only one or two pitches.

The Mark of Royalty

Trumpeters during the 1300s and 1400s were employed as tower watchmen for the city or royal courts, announcing danger and the arrival of guests. It was during this era that trumpets began to be used for church and popular music.

Because the earliest trumpets were more than six feet long and tended to bend from their own weight, the trumpet began to undergo a change in appearance. Around 1400, trumpet makers learned to bend metal tubing without compressing the metal in the area of the bend. The tubing could then be bent in thirds and shaped into a long "S," making the trumpet somewhat easier to carry and play.

Helpful Crooks

Trumpets during the Renaissance period (1400–1600) were pitched in a single key. In terms of your own modern instrument, it would be as though you could play only the notes on a single valve, several of which would be either quite sharp or quite flat.

With the invention of added crooks (lengths of tube coiled into various shapes), which were placed on the curve of the "S," trumpets could now be pitched in several keys to correspond to the music being played. In modern terms, this would mean you were still limited to a single fingering, but between pieces you could change which fingering it was! Nuremburg, Germany, became the center of trumpet making during this time.

It was during the Renaissance that trumpet music began to be written down, rather than just improvised. For example, Claudio Monteverdi included five trumpets in the opening music of his opera Orfeo! Trumpeters might be court musicians, playing more complex, notated music; or they might live and work outside the court, playing simple, traditional music for public gatherings.

The early part of the seventeenth century saw the formation of the trumpet guild, or Trompeterkameraschaft, which can be loosely equated with the modern musician's union. The guilds were intended to separate the town and court musicians, reserving certain musical functions for guild members alone to play.

Baroque Trumpet and Clarino Virtuosi

A new style of playing came to the fore during the Baroque period (1685–1750), inspiring a flurry of writing by such composers as Bach, Handel, Torelli, Telemann, Purcell, Manfredini, and Franceschini.

This new development centered on the fact that the notes in the extreme high range of the early trumpet are spaced closer together, so melodies and even short scales are possible in this range. Up to this time, most trumpet parts consisted of only a few notes in lower registers.

Composers increasingly began to take advantage of this higher register, or clarino; however, it required a very skillful trumpeter to play these notes accurately. Clarino players specialized in these higher passages, while other players performed the lower part, called the principale.

Hummel, Haydn, and the Keyed Trumpet

The trumpet went through a decline during the classical era (1750–1825), as Baroque trumpet concertos and fanfares seemed too old-fashioned. With music becoming increasingly harmonically complex, composers such as Mozart and Beethoven favored instruments that could play chromatically (all the notes in the scale, including half-steps).

Two concertos were written during the classical era that became standard solo literature for the trumpet: the concertos by Franz Joseph Haydn and Johann Nepomuk Hummel. Both concertos were written for a keyed trumpet invented by Anton Weidinger, and they were premiered in the early 1800s.

The keyed trumpet was the first trumpet that could perform chromatically. The invention of this trumpet—and the concertos written for it—marked a turning point in the history of brass instruments.

Valves' Grand Sweep

In 1818 the invention of the valve, patented by Heinrich Stolzel and Friedrich Blühmel, signaled the birth of the modern trumpet. Over the next thirty years, valves continued to develop, including the rotary valve, invented by Blühmel in 1828 (used on French horns and rotary trumpets), and the modern piston valve, invented by Étienne François Perinet in 1839.

Orchestral compositions now began to use the trumpet for more melodic passages, rather than reserving it only for fanfares. The cornet enjoyed the spotlight as the favored solo instrument during the nineteenth century, while the trumpet was used primarily as an orchestral instrument.

In the 1940s the trumpet began to surpass the cornet in popularity, with the rise of "big band" performers such as Benny Goodman and Harry James. The B♭ trumpet is most often used in bands, while the brighter C trumpet is preferred for orchestral playing.

The *tuning slide* is used to adjust the overall pitch of your trumpet. Pulling out this slide will lower the sound of every note on the trumpet (Figures 1.7 and 1.8). You may remove this slide without pressing any valves.

The tuning slide and second valve slide are considered "slow" slides since you do not use them while playing; the first and third valve slides are considered "fast" slides, since you use them to make rapid adjustments while playing.

To lubricate your slow slides, use slide grease or petroleum jelly. If you need your tuning slide to move more freely, you can add a drop or two of valve oil. The second valve slide is moved only when you are cleaning the instrument;

IMPORTANT: Never remove the first, second, or third slide on the trumpet without depressing the valve of the slide you are removing.

If you forget, the air pressure you have released will create a "pop" and the metal will expand rapidly. Over time, the expansion will become noticeable, and the slide will no longer make a proper seal.

The tuning slide may be moved freely without the need to depress any valves, because it is already open at the mouthpiece.

FIGURE 1.7

Pull out the main tuning slide to lower the trumpet's pitch.

FIGURE 1.8

Pull the main tuning slide toward you to raise the pitch.

it should receive only enough grease to protect the raw brass ends of the tubing, and to prevent it from becoming stuck.

If your fast slides already move freely, use valve oil to make them even faster. If they are a bit stiff, use grease instead, mixed with a few drops of oil, to loosen them up.

14

Lubricate your slides when they are dry to the touch, or whenever you clean your instrument. Use grease only on the raw brass part of the slide, not on the inside of the tube or on the finish. To minimize the grease that squeezes out when the slide is reinserted, apply only a thin film; use a rag to remove the excess.

Meet Your Mouthpiece

And now, the moment you have been waiting for.

You are about to meet your mouthpiece—the part of your trumpet that you will come to know better than any other. It will become in some ways an extension of you, one with your lips and your breath.

Of course, for now you probably just want to know how to insert it. Place the stem of your mouthpiece in the mouthpiece receiver, located at the top portion of the leadpipe. Give it a gentle turn to set it.

There is a bit more you should know about your mouthpiece in order to make sure that the mouthpiece you have is the one that is right for you. A mouthpiece has four key physical dimensions (Figure 1.9), each of which has a specific influence on your playing and sound. The rim, cup, cup diameter, and throat (backbore) are the primary dimensions used to compare mouthpieces.

1. **Rim**—A wide rim is very comfortable to play but requires the player to have greater lip strength to move between notes.

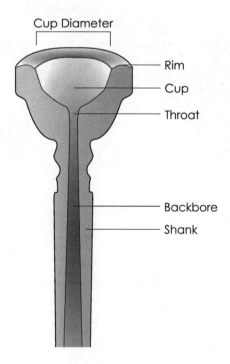

FIGURE 1.9

Dimensions of a mouthpiece

A narrower rim will offer more flexibility but won't cushion your lips as well.

2. **Cup**—The deeper the cup, the more easily you can reach lower notes. A shallower cup will produce a bright sound and a rapid response; a deeper cup will produce a deep, warm sound but will respond a little more slowly.

3. **Cup diameter**—A larger cup diameter (for example, a Bach 1C mouthpiece) will create a full, warm sound, but requires a very strong embouchure ("AHM-buh-sher," mouth shape and facial muscles used to play the instrument). The opposite is true for a smaller cup diameter (for example, a Bach 12C mouthpiece).

4. **Throat/Backbore**—Bore simply means the diameter of a tube. A larger throat will produce a rounder, more mellow sound, while a smaller throat will produce a brighter sound. If the throat is too large, it will result in a tendency to play flat (too low), and diminished endurance and range. If the throat is too small, the result will be poor tone quality, reduced range, and a tendency to play sharp (too high).

If you are a beginner, a great mouthpiece to start with is a Bach 7C or equivalent. This mouthpiece is at the midpoint in both size and depth. If your lip size is in the average range, this mouthpiece will allow you to develop good lip and embouchure control. If your lips are especially narrow or full, see "Embouchure and Lips: Finding the Perfect Marriage" (page 39) for some tips on accommodating your particular needs. Be sure to consult your teacher when making your choice.

The mouthpiece sizes above refer to the Bach brand. If your mouthpiece is numbered differently, refer to the Mouthpiece Comparison Chart on page 213.

Ten Commandments to Protect Your Trumpet

1. Never leave your trumpet where it could get stolen, stepped on or lost. Whether at home or at school, always store your instrument in a safe place.

2. Open your trumpet case on the floor, whether you are at home or at school. If you open the case on your lap, someone may walk by and accidentally knock your trumpet on the floor, leading to an expensive repair.

3. Brush your teeth before you play. Besides keeping your trumpet sanitary, this will prevent buildup that will change your trumpet's pitch, sound, and responsiveness.

4. Examine your instrument every time you take it out of the case so that you can immediately identify any new dents, scratches, or damage and respond appropriately.

5. Keep your mouthpiece clean. The mouthpiece is the first place that your air, saliva, and bacteria reach, and for that reason, it's often the dirtiest! Run lukewarm water through your mouthpiece and clean it with a mouthpiece brush.

6. When you set your trumpet down, place it on the side opposite the second valve slide to avoid accidental damage to the second valve slide or casing.

7. NEVER stand your trumpet on the bell. It can fall over easily, resulting in major repairs.

8. Wipe down your trumpet with a soft cloth after every practice and performance. Your trumpet's finish will last longer when you remove the acids and oils that are in your perspiration.

9. Clean the leadpipe of your trumpet after playing each day to reduce gritty deposits in the trumpet. Buy a silk clarinet swab and keep it in your case for this purpose (page 54).

10. If your mouthpiece gets stuck in the instrument, never try to remove it yourself. Take it to a music store and let a professional get it out. Band directors often have the tool to remove mouthpieces as well. Never use a wrench, pliers, or any tool that may damage your trumpet.

Posture and Placement

Ever notice how the people who get things done in life often carry themselves a certain way? They walk tall, move gracefully and easily, and speak with assurance. Achieving noteworthy results in life can start with simply holding yourself with confidence. In trumpet playing, it's an absolute requirement.

Your posture will affect your sound, endurance, concentration, and agility. A great set-up will start you on the path to excellent playing.

Placing the Left Hand

1. Set the instrument in your lap with the second valve slide facing down and the bell pointing to the left.
2. Place your ring finger (third finger) of your left hand in the third valve slide ring (Figure 2.1). (You can adjust the position of this ring on most beginner trumpets.)
3. Wrap your first two fingers around the third valve section.
4. Rest the thumb in the saddle, or wrap it around the first valve section.
5. Rest your pinky between the pipes of the third valve slide, or by the third valve slide ring.

Keep your hand somewhat relaxed, just firm enough to stabilize the trumpet. If your hold is too limp, the trumpet will shift while you're playing. However, keep your wrist relaxed, and don't squeeze!

FIGURE 2.1

Correct left hand placement

Right Hand and Fingers

The right hand is used only for balance and fingering. Your right hand should form a backward "C."

1. Place the tip of your thumb under the leadpipe, between the first and second valve sections (Figure 2.2).
2. Place the pads of your first three fingers on the finger buttons (Figure 2.3).
3. Place your right pinky finger on top of the pinky ring, or simply let it move freely (Figure 2.4). In spite of its name, the pinky ring is used only for one-handed page turns, or when your other hand is working a mute.

When fingering, make sure the pads of your fingers remain in contact with the finger buttons; don't lift them for each note. You can place pennies between your fingers and the finger buttons when you practice, to keep you from forgetting!

FIGURE 2.2

Correct right hand placement

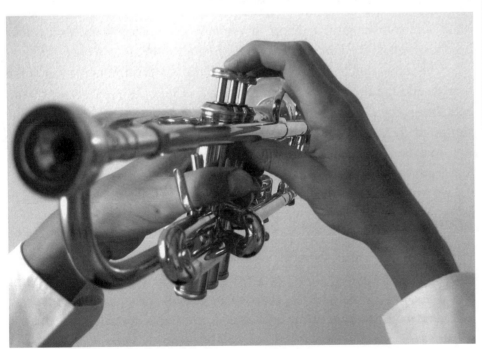

FIGURE 2.3

Correct hand position from the player's point of view

FIGURE 2.4

Placing the right pinky

Head, Arms, and Shoulders

Make sure you bring the trumpet to you, not vice versa. Do not thrust your head forward; it is bad for your neck and will limit your airflow.

Your arms should form a triangle, with the wrists forming the top of the triangle and the two elbows forming the base (Figure 2.5). The valves should be either perpendicular to the floor, or tilted slightly to the right from your viewpoint, for ease of fingering.

Make sure your elbows are away from your body, allowing your chest area to expand.

Trumpet Angle and Seated Posture

When you sit to play the trumpet, every aspect of your body will be supporting your sound and contributing in a positive way to your playing. A great seated posture not only looks professional, but also raises your energy level and contributes to your focus and attitude during rehearsals and concerts (Figure 2.6).

FIGURE 2.5

Arms form a triangle

When you play, your head should be balanced, relaxed, and centered, with the top of your head relatively flat and your chin approximately parallel to the floor. If you have a slight overbite (and most people do), your trumpet should be at a slight downward slope. A player may occasionally raise the bell for a solo, but this angle would be too high for ordinary playing (Figure 2.7), while an angle that is too low will result in a pinched sound (Figure 2.8).

Place your feet flat on the ground, shoulder-width apart, and sit forward on your chair, with your back at least six inches from the back of the chair. Your

FIGURE 2.6

Correct seated posture

knees should form a 90-degree angle. Girls, remember that you cannot cross your legs when you play, so you might want to save the short skirts for days when you don't have band!

Lift and lengthen your spine to allow your rib cage to expand. If your air column is relaxed, your sound will be full and rich and breathing will be easier. Keeping your body balanced when you play will minimize back and shoulder pain and allow you to perform better.

Slouching during rehearsal not only affects your sound but communicates that you are not interested in what you are doing (Figure 2.9). This creates a

23

FIGURE 2.7

This angle is too high for ordinary playing. The bell should be angled slightly downward.

FIGURE 2.8

An angle that is too low will result in a pinched sound.

24

FIGURE 2.9

Slouching during rehearsal will diminish both your sound and your energy.

negative environment for both others and yourself! While maintaining good posture may initially require strengthening new muscles, in a short time you'll be able to effortlessly maintain excellent form.

Placing the Music Stand

For orchestra and band playing, your trumpet should be held to the side of the music stand, so that your sound is not obstructed (Figure 2.10).

If you position your music stand far enough away, you may play directly toward it (Figure 2.11). However, make sure you can still see the conductor, make eye contact with other musicians, and easily read the music.

In a jazz ensemble, the trumpet bell may be placed above a very low stand for sound production. This is the traditional placement for big band.

In any case, make sure you don't block your sound by playing either into the music stand or toward the floor. Playing into the music stand will muffle your sound and flatten your pitch, while playing into the floor will bury your sound under everyone's chairs!

Standing to Perform

If you are standing to perform, place your feet shoulder-width apart (Figure 2.12). Gently lift and lengthen your spine to open your air column. Never lean backward; if anything, lean a little forward.

FIGURE 2.10

Place your bell to the right of the music stand, to allow the sound to project

FIGURE 2.11

You may play directly into the music stand as long as it is placed far enough from your bell.

As all choir members know, it is important to keep your knees slightly bent! Locking your knees can eventually cause you to pass out.

When practicing, make sure your stand is high enough to encourage an energetic, lifted posture.

FIGURE 2.12

When standing to play, stand straight or lean slightly forward.

Trumpet Posture Points

Good Posture Means . . .

Head set on top of the spine

Straight, relaxed, and supported back positioned six inches from the
back of the chair

Feet flat on the floor

Chin parallel to the floor or slightly tucked

Trumpet at a slight downward slope, 10 to 30 degrees below level

Shoulders relaxed and dropped; elbows away from the body

Watch Out for . . .

Head thrust forward

Droopy shoulders

Curved back

Crossed legs

Knees locked while standing

Slouched seating posture

Besides affecting your sound, incorrect posture may lead to chronic hand,
neck or back pain, in addition to tendon and nerve damage over years of
playing.

Buzz to Brilliance

Every afternoon the sounds of Maynard Ferguson and his band penetrated the walls of my bedroom. The band sound was a wave of brass power that slammed into you, with beats that made your soul vibrate.

Maynard Ferguson played higher than any other trumpeter I had ever heard. I could not understand how someone could play so high and make it sound so easy!

Embouchure refers to the way a player's muscles and soft tissue form around the mouthpiece of a wind instrument. The word comes from the French *bouche,* meaning "mouth." The embouchure is where the magic happens in trumpet playing, allowing you to reach those vaulting high notes, or leaving you stuck and frustrated on the ground!

To prepare your embouchure for the mouthpiece, follow these steps:

1. Make the sound "emmm." Use the muscles at the corners of your mouth to pull your lips somewhat taut.
2. This formation will pull your lips back against your four top teeth and four bottom teeth. These teeth will help physically reinforce the correct embouchure.
3. Make sure your top lip doesn't overlap your bottom lip; they should be even. Don't turn your corners up into a smile, or allow your lips to pucker outward.
4. Now, anchor your corners (prevent them from moving) to stabilize your embouchure. You might imagine the muscles just below your mouth helping firm your corners.

Break Out the Buzz

Getting a sound on the trumpet isn't about simply moving air through it—as you will quickly discover if you form your lips over the mouthpiece and blow air through the trumpet. You will, in fact, hear a sound . . . the rushing of air! When you play the trumpet, the air you blow matters only because it carries your lips' vibrations, or buzz, which is then amplified inside the trumpet.

With your embouchure set, the next step is to create your buzz—which will soon unleash your trumpet playing on the world.

1. Set the embouchure using the "emmm" formation (Figure 3.1).
2. Wet the inside of your lips.
3. Imagine that you are holding an M&M in the center of your lips
4. Blow a narrow, fast stream of air through the center of your lips, where you are holding the imaginary M&M. Your lips should vibrate the way they would if you were to imitate a half-full balloon leaking air.

If you can't get your lips to vibrate, first try using faster air! If this doesn't work, you may need to firm your corners, or you may even need to relax your

FIGURE 3.1

Set your embouchure using an "emmm" formation. Notice the firm corners.

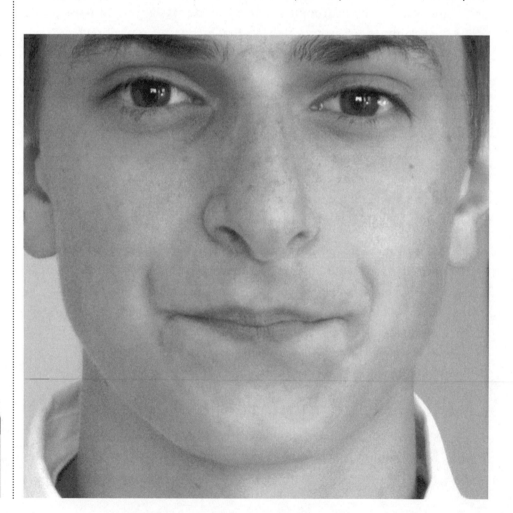

30

lips slightly. Make sure your lips are aligned (you might need to bring your lower jaw slightly forward). Some players find it helpful to keep the lips slightly rolled in, particularly if the bottom lip wants to buckle outward.

Only One Way Out

Your aperture (Figure 3.2) is the opening in your lips that is created when the fast airstream pushes your lips apart. It is shown here inside the ring of a mouthpiece visualizer, a tool that helps you see where to place your mouthpiece on your lips.

If you place your index fingers on both sides of your aperture, you will notice that the soft tissue of the lips on the sides of the aperture is vibrating, but there is no air moving through the lips at this point. Your two index fingers are right now stabilizing this area much as the mouthpiece will do, helping you keep the vibration in the center of the lips.

When you firm the center of your embouchure and move air through your lips, the air won't blow your lips open quite as far. The resulting aperture will be smaller, and the resulting pitch higher. To lower the pitch, you will loosen the center of your embouchure. You will notice your jaw raising and lowering slightly, but the movement should be extremely subtle.

The tightening and loosening of the embouchure is the first of two elements that together are used to raise and lower the pitch on the trumpet. Before we learn the second, we are going to introduce your lips to the mouthpiece.

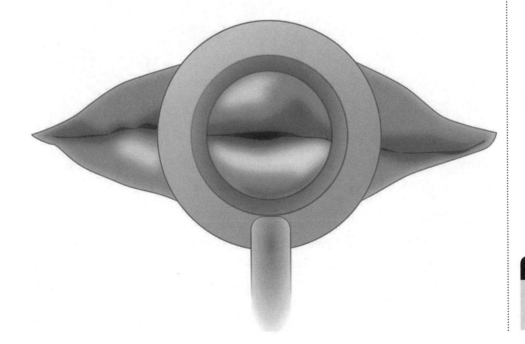

FIGURE 3.2

The aperture is the football-shaped opening in the center of the lips.

32

Adding the Metal

When setting your mouthpiece onto your embouchure, hold the mouthpiece by the shank about an inch from the end, using the thumb and two fingers of your non-dominant hand (Figure 3.3). You will be less likely to exert excess pressure with this hand.

FIGURE 3.3

Hold the mouthpiece with the thumb and two fingers of your non-dominant hand.

Next, place the mouthpiece on your top lip first, to anchor it. By doing this, you are providing the mouthpiece with a firm position on your upper jaw (which is part of the cranium), while the hinged lower jaw can make any necessary adjustments. Make sure the mouthpiece is centered on your lips both horizontally and vertically, and that the outer rim rests on the skin above and below the lips (Figure 3.4).

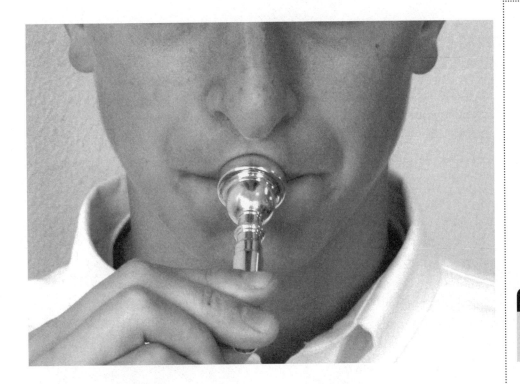

FIGURE 3.4

Correct placement of embouchure on the trumpet mouthpiece.

Since most players have a slight overbite, the trumpet will typically be most comfortable at a slight downward angle. This means your airflow should be slightly downward as well. Some players (especially those with irregular dental surfaces) may need to adjust their mouthpiece position in other ways; if this is you, see "Embouchure and Lips: Finding the Perfect Marriage," page 39.

Once you are able to accurately place your mouthpiece, you are ready for the last step.

Create a good lip buzz; then, with your lip buzz still going, bring your mouthpiece to your embouchure.

Voilà! You have buzzed your first note on the mouthpiece.

Six Points for a Good Embouchure

1. Center the mouthpiece vertically and horizontally on your lips.
2. Keep your jaw in a natural, slightly dropped position. It should feel relaxed and steady.
3. Maintain firm corners.
4. Keep your tongue down and out of the way of your air stream.
5. Keep the aperture in the center of the lips.
6. Work with a mirror at all times.

Embouchure Pitfalls

Watch out for any of these six signs, which will tell you that your embouchure or mouthpiece placement needs some attention!

1. **"Smile" embouchure**
   If you appear to be smiling while buzzing on your mouthpiece, your corners are pulled back too far, stretching out your lips (Figure 1). The result will be poor range and poor flexibility (ability to move between notes using the lips).

Figure 1. "Smile" embouchure (incorrect). Notice how far the corners are pulled back.

2. **Bunched-up chin**
   Contracting the muscles in the chin will pull the corners downward and cause the bottom lip to protrude, resulting in poor range and flexibility (Figure 2).

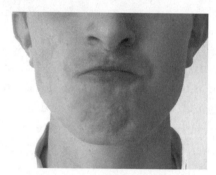

Figure 2. "Bunched-up chin" embouchure (incorrect). Notice how the bottom lip is rolled out and the corners are pulled downward.

3. **Mouthpiece too high or too low**
   The mouthpiece should be centered vertically, with half on the top lip and half on the bottom, so the mouthpiece pressure is equally distributed. Having your mouthpiece too high (Figure 3) or too low (Figure 4) can reduce your endurance and range.

Figure 3. Mouthpiece placed too high on the embouchure

4. **Mouthpiece not centered over the aperture**

   If your mouthpiece is not centered on your aperture (Figure 5), it will partially block the air as you blow. Ideally, your air stream should aim directly into the throat of the mouthpiece.

5. **Excessive pressure**

   Take it easy, and use only enough mouthpiece pressure to make a good seal with your lips! Embouchure damage from excessive pressure has prematurely ended the careers of many successful trumpeters.

6. **Puffed cheeks**

   Although some players have enjoyed successful professional careers playing with puffed cheeks, your volume comes from your breath support, not the air in your cheeks. Puffing your cheeks can make it difficult to maintain a good embouchure (Figure 6).

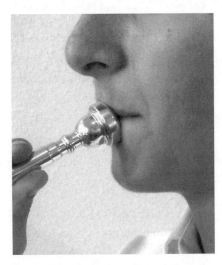

Figure 4. Mouthpiece placed too low on the embouchure

Figure 5. Mouthpiece is horizontally off center.

Figure 6. Make sure your cheeks do not puff out.

35

Work Your Chops with Your Buzz

Now is the moment to introduce the element that will aid the embouchure in raising and lowering the pitch. Ready? The answer is on the tip of your tongue.

Well, actually, the answer *is* your tongue.

The tongue is a very unusual muscle; unlike other muscles, it is attached only at one end! You have already spent years raising and lowering it when you whistle—although you've probably never noticed how you were making those pitch changes. You will use your tongue in a similar way to support your note changes on the trumpet.

1. Create a good lip buzz, following the steps on page 30.
2. Bring the mouthpiece to your lips while you are buzzing, using only enough pressure to create a good air seal. The mouthpiece will serve as a resonator for the buzz, creating a note.
3. Sustain the note for 4–8 seconds, working to stabilize your tone.
4. To raise the pitch, tighten your embouchure and slightly raise, or arch, your tongue.
5. To lower the pitch, slightly relax your embouchure and lower your tongue.

Use a hand mirror to check your embouchure. Your jaw may move subtly as you tighten and loosen your embouchure, but the movement should be slight.

You ultimately want a single aperture in the center of the lips, with everything from the edge of the aperture through the corners of the mouth sealed and firmly set. However, it is normal not to be able to achieve this initially! If your lips are vibrating in two or three places, it simply means your muscles are weak. After a few days you will be able to keep the vibration in the center.

Breaths of "Oo!" and "Oh!"

Not just gasps of amazement anymore, "oo" and "oh," together with "ee," will serve now as a guide for your tongue position. When you play notes in the middle register, your tongue is in the "oo" position (Figure 3.5). We will consider this the resting position of the tongue.

Your tongue will lower as the notes descend, and for the lowest notes (below the C just below the staff) your tongue will be in an "oh" position (Figure 3.6). The larger size of the oral cavity allows you to reliably hit the lower notes.

For higher notes (above high G on the staff), your tongue will be in the "ee" position (Figure 3.7). Raising the tongue decreases the size of the oral cavity; the resonance of this smaller space is a match for the frequency of the high notes, helping you to reliably hit these notes.

"Embouchure is just 10 percent of trumpet playing. But that 10 percent has got to be 100 percent right."

— William Adam

36

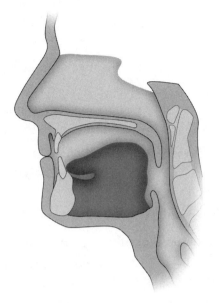

FIGURE 3.5

Tongue position for the "oo" vowel

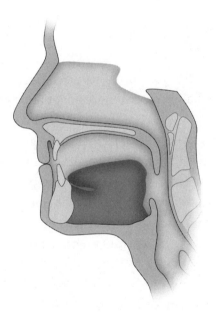

FIGURE 3.6

Tongue position for the "oh" vowel

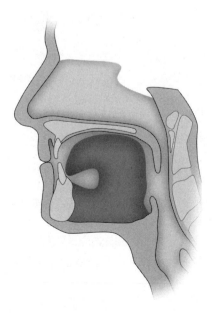

FIGURE 3.7

Tongue position for the "ee" vowel

Use the following exercises to practice your tongue and embouchure coordination:

1. Buzz a siren sound, rising and falling. See how high and low you can get.
2. Once you have achieved a good siren, buzz a short scale, raising the pitch step by step. Move cleanly from note to note, making sure the pitch does not bend.
3. Play two notes on the piano, then try to find the same notes on your mouthpiece.
4. Buzz some simple, familiar melodies.

Buzzing on your mouthpiece is the beginning of excellent trumpet technique! Before you actually begin playing the instrument, you will be perfecting your buzzing for a few weeks, building your muscles and getting used to the way the mouthpiece fits on your lips.

The Perfect Lips

To get a good vibration with your lips, they need to be loose and supple. Over time your lips will gradually become more adept at producing and sustaining your buzz.

Most brass players avoid wearing lip balm, lip gloss, or lipstick when they play. Besides interfering with your playing surface, these will also tend to leave a residue on your mouthpiece. If there is a product you like to use, that's fine—just carry tissues with you so you can wipe it off before you play, then balm your lips to your heart's content once your practice is finished.

As you develop your buzz and your embouchure, take your time with the details! It will take longer to kick bad habits than it would have taken to learn correctly the first time. In this case, unlearning bad habits also means retraining your muscles—a double whammy. Use a hand mirror or locker mirror—clipped to the stand if possible—to check each aspect of your mouthpiece placement and embouchure.

You might ask your teacher or director if they have a mouthpiece visualizer you can use. The mouthpiece visualizer is an open rim with a metal rod connected to it. While holding the metal rod with your hand, place the rim of the visualizer on your embouchure (Figure 3.8) and look into a mirror to see if your aperture is directly centered.

Watch your embouchure carefully over your first several weeks of practice. A few weeks of working with a mirror on your stand are worth it to avoid struggling with a bad habit for years! Consult your teacher if you're not sure everything is working well—especially if your mouthpiece placement is atypical because of your lip or dental characteristics. Your teachers have worked with many students and can give you tips that make a big difference.

Embouchure and Lips: Finding the Perfect Marriage

If you are someone with irregular teeth or lip shape, don't worry! Some great players have major idiosyncrasies for which they've compensated by making intelligent changes in their mouthpiece placement. Changes can be made to the vertical position, the horizontal position (left-to-right), or the angle of the mouthpiece.

Fuller or Thinner Lips

If you have very full lips, you will need to roll your lips in a bit more when forming the "emmm" position to place your mouthpiece. You want the mouthpiece to sit on the outer portion of your lips as much as possible. You may be more comfortable using a mouthpiece with a wider cup diameter and a deeper cup, such as the Bach 5B mouthpiece.

If you have extremely thin lips (not much lip surface at all), you may be more comfortable using a mouthpiece with a smaller cup diameter, such as the Bach 10½ C. As your embouchure grows stronger, you will move to a mouthpiece with a larger cup diameter.

Dental Irregularities

If you have an overbite, your trumpet angle will have to be slightly more downward than is typical, so the air stream can directly enter the throat of the mouthpiece. Otherwise, your air column will hit the inner cup of the mouthpiece, causing intonation and range problems.

If one of your front teeth protrudes slightly, you will want to place your mouthpiece over the center of that tooth. This may be a little left or right of center. Ask an experienced teacher to help you find the perfect placement for you.

Working with a Teardrop Lip

Some people have a bit of extra flesh, or "teardrop," that hangs down from the center of the top lip. Although a teardrop lip is not preferred for trumpeters, you and your teacher can work around this lovely idiosyncrasy so that it doesn't get in the way of your playing.

To start with, use a mouthpiece with a wider and flatter outer rim, such as the Schilke 13C4. This rim is wide enough that even when placed in the standard position on the embouchure, a bit of the rim will press into the

39

teardrop and hold it in place, damping its vibration. Have your teacher show you how to correctly roll in your lip to minimize the vibration of the teardrop. You may also try placing the mouthpiece slightly left or right of center—whichever is more comfortable—to help isolate the teardrop and keep it from vibrating.

If you have a teardrop lip, you will definitely want to work with a good trumpet teacher throughout your study, to address issues as they arise!

Wet or Dry?

Brass players keep the inside of the aperture moist at all times, because it allows the lips to vibrate more freely. So what does someone mean when they talk about playing with a "wet set" or "dry set"?

Playing with a "wet set" refers not only to the inside of the aperture but also to lips and the skin just around them. Playing with this area moist feels smooth and soft, allows you to make small adjustments in the placement of the mouthpiece when needed, and can be helpful until you settle into a good embouchure. To play with a wet set, lick the entire area where the mouthpiece will be placed, or lick the mouthpiece before placing it on your lips.

The advantage of playing with a "dry set" is greater security while playing, since the mouthpiece is not free to move around once put into place. In general, playing with a dry set is preferable for seasoned players. However, someone whose skin is particularly sensitive to the friction of the mouthpiece might find that using a wet set eliminates this problem.

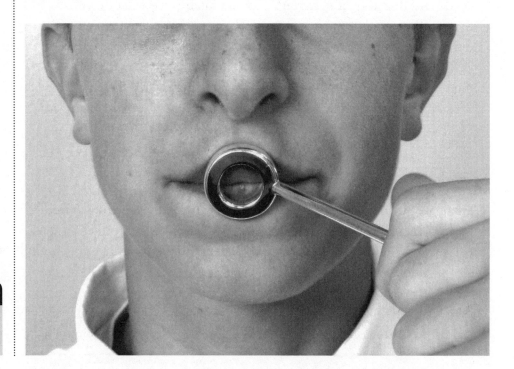

FIGURE 3.8

Correct placement of the embouchure on the mouthpiece visualizer

Chapped Lips

Chapped lips can be a persistent problem for brass players, since we tend to moisten our lips more often than other wind players do. Dry winter air can exacerbate chapping. Take excellent care of your lips at all times, and treat chapped lips as a minor injury that deserves your attention.

To preserve your lips' health, try not to moisten them when you're not actually playing. Licking your lips may feel good for a few minutes, but in the long run it will dry them out more. Drink plenty of water, since your body will pull moisture from the skin when you're dehydrated.

To treat chapped lips, break open a vitamin E capsule and rub it over your lips until they absorb the oil. Before you go to sleep, apply either lip balm or petroleum jelly so your lips can heal during the night. Avoid lip balms that have the active ingredients camphor and menthol, which actually dry the lips. Some people are also sensitive to petroleum jelly. Consider using a balm with natural ingredients such as cocoa butter, shea butter, almond oil, or something similar.

Treat your lips with a balm frequently until they heal, and use lip balm as needed to prevent the dryness from recurring.

Now . . . to the Trumpet!

You will spend lots of time buzzing and learning to control your lips before playing on the trumpet itself. Expect to spend about three weeks (a few private lessons) practicing your pitch and rhythm while buzzing your mouthpiece, beginning to train and strengthen your embouchure. Once you have a great buzz, you'll be able to play the trumpet in no time!

Basics on the Trumpet

I t was a phonograph record of Wynton Marsalis playing the Haydn and Hummel trumpet concertos. I found it in the stacks of records in my dad's music library, and it was unlike anything I'd heard in my life. Wynton's crystalline sound and artistic turns of phrase made his trumpet sound like pure magic. I played that record so often that even the needle on my record player knew every note from memory.

The Haydn concerto was on the first side of the album. I didn't have the music, so I tried to figure it out by ear. One day I came home and found the music waiting on my bed. It was like having the answer key to a test! I learned the whole piece in a month.

Now that you and your trumpet are beginning to know each other, you might be looking for some answer keys of your own. For example, perhaps you're asking, "Why does my tuner say B♭ when I'm supposed to be playing a C?" and "How do you clean this thing?"

This chapter is designed to answer some of the questions you may have at this point . . . and perhaps to answer a few others before you come up with them.

A Note by Any Other Name

If you are particularly ambitious and have already played a few notes on your trumpet with the new and exciting tuner you picked up at the music store, you may have discovered something dismaying.

44

The tuner seems to have an unexpected malfunction. Whenever you play a C, the tuner displays a B♭. Whenever you play a G, it displays an F.

The tuner seems to be operating according to some peculiar logic . . . which would be fine, except that electronic gadgets are not supposed to have minds of their own.

Don't worry; your tuner isn't broken, and neither is your trumpet—or you. While most instruments in the orchestra play at concert pitch—that is, the note on the page is the note that is produced—most brass instruments are transposing instruments. For a transposing instrument, the music is adjusted depending on the instrument being played. This allows the performer to play the same printed note using the same fingering, whether they are playing a trumpet, a piccolo trumpet, or even a flugelhorn.

Your music should read "Trumpet in B♭," which signifies that it has been adjusted for you. As you read your music, the note that comes out on your B♭ instrument will always be one full step below what's printed on the page. You can still pick up a piece of piano music and play it, and it will sound perfectly fine. Just don't have your sister play it on the piano along with you—unless your goal is to give your parents a headache!

Later in your study you will learn to adjust for music that hasn't already been adjusted for you. This skill is called transposition.

One Valve, Several Notes

With three valves on the trumpet, there are seven possible fingerings, including "open" (no valves pressed). Since, clearly, there are more than seven notes on a piano—or, for that matter, in any trumpet solo from a John Philip Sousa march—it follows that each fingering must produce several notes. The way to get additional notes for each fingering is to tighten or loosen the embouchure and change the height of your tongue.

Your beginner book will start you playing on a written G (the second line on the staff) or low C (the line just below the staff). These notes are both played open (without pressing down valves). Some beginners find it easier to play the C, while others find G easier. The note that is initially easier for you is considered your *natural note*.

Once you can get both of these notes by changing your embouchure and tongue height, experiment with various fingerings (pressing down the valves) and use your embouchure and tongue height to find various notes on each new fingering. You may be surprised by how many notes you can now play! After you have experimented for awhile, choose one note and try to play it consistently on the first try.

Yet More Harmonics

It may occasionally seem that whenever you go to play a particular note on the trumpet, a half dozen other notes seem ready to come out instead of the one you're looking for! You may remember playing a particular handheld game featuring a flat disc with small holes in it and an equal number of small beads. The task is to tilt the toy until each bead is resting in a hole. The little balls seem to have a mind of their own . . . kind of like the notes on your trumpet.

The harmonic series is the group of notes produced by a single source of vibration. When you strike a bell, for example, it vibrates at many different frequencies, all at the same time. These vibrations all blend together into a sound, and we hear the loudest frequency, or vibration, as one particular note. The loudness or softness of each frequency within the overall, blended sound is what makes each instrument unique, giving each instrument its *timbre* ("TAM-ber"), which allows us to tell an oboe from a violin, or a trumpet from a French horn—even when they are playing the same note.

As you can guess, the harmonic series is also what determines the set of notes that can be produced on each trumpet fingering.

Each trumpet fingering can produce a very low note, another note eight steps higher (the first harmonic), another note five steps higher than that (the second harmonic), and so on. The pattern is the same for each fingering.

Your aperture and tongue height together determine which of these possible notes (or harmonics) you actually produce. As you can see from the illustration below (Figure 4.1), the notes on a single fingering cover quite a range.

FIGURE 4.1

The harmonic series is the group of notes that can all be produced on a particular trumpet fingering. This harmonic series is for the trumpet fingered "open" (no valves).

One More Moving Part

As though it wasn't enough to get all those little beads to rest in their respective holes, there is one more trick you will need in order to to play some notes correctly.

Due to some idiosyncrasies in the physics of the trumpet, a few notes on the trumpet play slightly sharp. To correct these notes, you will use your left-hand ring finger, resting in the third valve slide ring, to extend the slide as you play (Figures 4.2 and 4.3).

46

When extending your third valve slide, the movement should be a rapid flick that is simultaneous with the valve press. Quickly pull the slide back in while moving to the next note. If the movement is too slow, you will actually hear the pitch slide downward or upward—an inelegant way to proceed from note to note! Don't push or pull too hard; the jarring motion may create a wobble in your sound. The better lubricated your slide is, the more easily it will move.

"Using the Third Valve Slide" shows the notes that you will play using the third valve slide. You should consider the third valve slide to be part of the fingering for these notes.

If the third valve slide does not move freely, it probably just needs slide grease. If you've applied grease and it still doesn't move, it is probably bent and misaligned, and will need to be professionally repaired (see chapter 17).

Please don't try to fix a stuck slide yourself; there is a good chance you will further damage your trumpet. An experienced repair person has things you don't have—such as tools and . . . well . . . experience.

Puzzling Out the Notes

A trumpet player must be able to remember what each note sounds like, since the correct fingering gets you only part of the way there! As you learn the songs in your beginning book, listen to yourself and notice how high or low each note sounds.

If you're not sure which note you're playing, get out your tuner. Remember that your tuner assumes that you're playing an instrument at concert pitch.

> *"I found that the more I practiced, the better I played, and the better I played, the more I enjoyed it."*
>
> —Adolph "Bud" Herseth

47

TABLE 4.1 Using the Third Valve Slide

Fingering	Note	Tendency	Correction
1-3		Sharp	Extend third valve slide*
		Sharp	Extend third valve slide
1-2-3		Very sharp	Extend third valve slide. This note is more sharp than D and requires a greater adjustment.
		Very sharp	Extend the third valve slide almost completely.

*While low G, fingered 1-3, is sharp in general, you may notice your low register is flat in general due to poor air support and a loose embouchure. To correct this, increase your air speed and tighten your embouchure slightly.

TABLE 4.2 Practicing with Your Tuner

B♭ Trumpet Note	Your Tuner Says
C	B♭
C♯	B
D	C
D♯ (or E♭)	C♯ (or D♭)
E	D
F	E♭
F♯	E
G	F
G♯ (or A♭)	F♯
A	G
A♯ (or B♭)	G♯ (or A♭)
B	A

When you play your "C," the screen will read "B♭." The chart on the next page may help you get more comfortable translating between the tuner and the printed note.

Good news! Some tuners have a transposing feature. Look for a button that shows the flat sign (♭). Push this button twice, and you will see two flats on the display. Now when you play your "C," the tuner will also read "C."

You will want to make sure, at this stage of your playing, that your main tuning slide is pushed out quite far; the actual distance will vary from person to person. As a beginner, your lips are naturally fairly tight, causing your pitch to be higher on all notes when you play. You will need to lower the pitch of your trumpet to compensate. As your lips become more supple over your first few years of study, your natural pitch will begin to drop and you'll push the tuning slide inward—shortening the length and raising the pitch—to compensate for your increasingly relaxed embouchure.

Out of Thin Air

So how are you supposed to get the right note each time, instead of another note on the same fingering?

Two things need to happen. You need to anticipate the sound of the correct note, and you need to reproduce how your embouchure felt when you played that note correctly last time around. When this skill becomes automatic, it is called muscle memory.

To begin developing your muscle memory, start by working with the notes fingered open. Pick one of these notes and see if you can hit it every single time. Now pick another note and do the same thing. Try to hear the correct pitch in your mind before you play it.

Next, build your consistency by alternating three of one note and three of the other note. Then do two of each, consciously trying to remember what each one feels like.

If you want to keep yourself amused while practicing this skill, create a game in which each correct note counts for one point. Try to get ten points in only fifteen tries. As you improve, see if you can get ten points in only twelve tries. Ultimately, your goal is ten for ten.

Surprises from Your Bell

Your sound isn't going to be everything you dreamed of right now, because your lips just can't pull that off yet. You won't necessarily get the correct note each time either! Don't worry—you'll get there soon enough. For the time being, there are a few specific sounds that you should pay attention to.

First, if you hear the sound of air leaking, make sure your embouchure is completely sealed and your corners are firm. This will become easier as your muscles become stronger and you can keep your aperture centered inside the mouthpiece.

If you are blowing through the trumpet with a good embouchure and no musical sound is coming out, you probably need faster air to get your aperture actually vibrating. It is also possible that your lips are too close together or too far apart. You need to find the position right in the middle, where the air causes them to vibrate against each other.

When players refer to cracking, splitting, or chipping a note, they are referring to those frustrating occasions when a couple different sounds come out just before you find the note you were looking for. Cracked notes are usually caused by (1) not enough air, (2) incorrect embouchure for that particular note, or (3) having your mouthpiece in the wrong place (especially if you just put your trumpet to your lips).

As you get tired, you may find that your tone is shaky and you are becoming inaccurate. If so, it's time to take a break from the instrument and return to it once the muscles are rested. If the tone becomes so distorted that it almost sounds like two notes are coming out, it means your lips are really fatigued! This phenomenon is called a double buzz, and happens when your top and bottom lip are vibrating at different speeds. If you hear a double buzz, it's time to give it a break for the day!

A Lesson from the Horses

Once you've been playing trumpet (or even just mouthpiece buzzing) for a few weeks, you may notice that after a long day of practice, or the next morning, your embouchure muscles are somewhat tight and unable to vibrate freely.

49

While it may not be the most dignified sound in the world, lip flapping is a great way to wake up the muscles and get rid of lactic acid buildup from your workout the day before.

To flap your lips, keep them very loose and imitate the sound a horse makes while shaking its head, or the sound of a helicopter. As your first warm-up exercise of the day, gently flap your lips for about 30 seconds. Next, mouthpiece buzz for twenty to thirty seconds and then lip flap again for about twenty seconds.

Once you are in a regular practice routine, you will alternate lip flapping and mouthpiece buzzing for four to five minutes, helping you ease into your practice in a way that protects your embouchure and increases your flexibility. As you progress in your playing, you will move toward the complete warm-up routine detailed in chapter 7, "Warm-Up and Warm-Down" (page 79).

Later in the year, when you begin to play longer songs, you will notice that the pressure from your mouthpiece will gradually push the blood out of your lips, eventually causing fatigue—even when you're not pressing too hard. During long rehearsals and performances (but not in the quiet moments!), flapping your lips will help get the blood and oxygen flowing back to your muscles so they are ready for more action.

Waterproof the Music

Of all the interesting sounds you might make on the trumpet, one is particularly charming . . . and, for once, has nothing to do with your embouchure.

As you buzz your lips into your trumpet, small amounts of saliva are released into the trumpet, and water vapor present in the air will condense in the instrument. That interesting gurgling sound as you play is a sign you need to empty your water keys.

Most beginner trumpets and cornets are equipped with a water key on both the main tuning slide and the third valve slide. Professional trumpets typically lack a water key on the third valve slide.

To get the water out of your trumpet, hold down the water key on the main tuning slide and press down all three valves (Figure 4.4). Close your lips over the mouthpiece and blow a gentle stream of air through the trumpet (Figure 4.5). Don't form your embouchure when you empty your water keys! You don't want to be responsible for an awkward honk from the trumpet section just as someone else is rounding off a lovely solo.

Once you have emptied your water using the water key on the main tuning slide, hold open the water key on the third slide (Figure 4.6). Press all three valves and blow.

If you are playing a cornet, there is one additional step. First, empty the water from both water keys by following the above steps. Then remove the main tuning slide of the cornet and shake it out. There will often be a good deal of water still hiding there.

FIGURE 4.4

Press down all three valves and open the water key on the main tuning slide.

FIGURE 4.5

Form your lips over the mouthpiece, without making an embouchure, and blow!

52

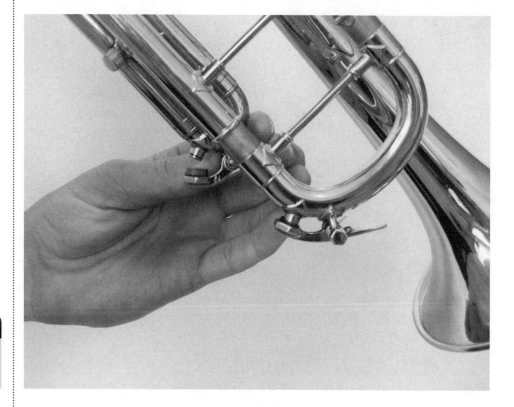

A side note . . . as a wind player, you may quickly get used to having a little water on the floor, but do be courteous with your puddles, especially when you are not in the band hall! Hold a cloth under your water key when you empty it, or clean up any puddles before you leave.

Leak in the Attic

If you've emptied both water keys and still hear gurgling as you play, some water may be left in the first, second, or third valve casing.

First, press the first valve and remove its slide. Hold the trumpet straight up and down and blow through the trumpet while pressing the first valve a few times. Replace this slide.

Next, press the second valve and remove its slide. Rotate the trumpet so the open tubes are pointed toward the floor (Figure 4.7). Press all the valves and blow through the trumpet; then hold the second valve down and press the first and third valves a few times while blowing through the trumpet. You should now be water-free.

On professional trumpets without a water key on the third valve slide, the third valve slide must be removed as well. Press the third valve, remove its slide,

FIGURE 4.7

Remove water from the first or second valve casing, if necessary.

and shake it lightly. With the slide removed and the trumpet angled downward, hold down all three valves and blow through the trumpet.

It's a Trumpet, Not a Petri Dish

Wherever there is water, there is life. In the case of your trumpet, that is not necessarily a good thing!

Before packing your trumpet in its case after each practice or performance, there are a few things you need to do to care for your instrument . . . and to avoid creating new ecosystems. If you leave water in there, you are encouraging bacteria, which, besides being unsanitary, will over time corrode the metal from the inside out. Always brush your teeth before you play to minimize particles and deposits in your trumpet.

For the best results, purchase a clarinet swab and run it through the leadpipe before you put the trumpet away, to dry any dampness remaining on the surface of the leadpipe. To do this, you will remove the tuning slide, drop the narrow end of the swab through the mouthpiece receiver (Figure 4.8) and pull the swab out the other end of the leadpipe (Figure 4.9). Repeat this process from the other direction.

54

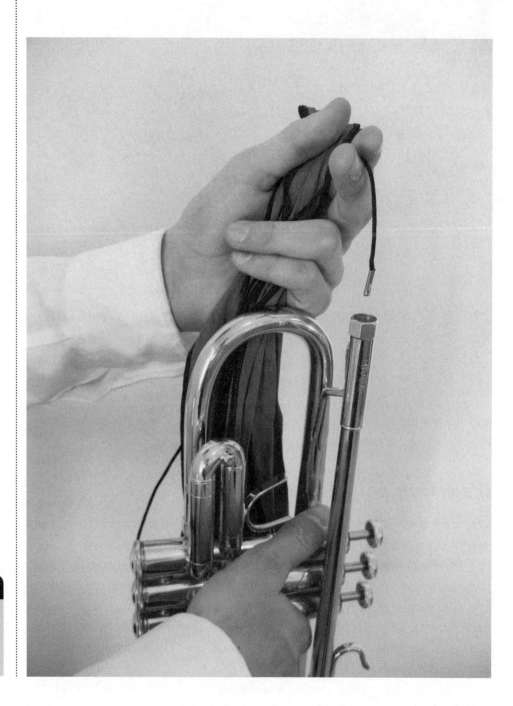

FIGURE 4.8

To clean your leadpipe, remove the tuning slide, then drop a clarinet swab into the mouthpiece receiver.

FIGURE 4.9

Pull the clarinet swab through the leadpipe, wrapping the loose fabric around your hand.

Exploring the Slides and Chutes

What the steam engine was to the horse and buggy, the piston valve was to the trumpet. Designed by the hornist Heinrich Stolzel in 1814, valves made every note of the scale available in the middle range of brass instruments, instead of just the handful of notes available previously.

Long Slides, Short Slides

Each valve opens a length of tubing that adds to the overall length of the trumpet. These tubes are called *valve slides*. The slides can be extended outward to fine-tune the notes, or removed completely for cleaning purposes.

Looking at the tubing pictured below, notice that the length of the first and second valve slides combined almost equals the length of the third valve slide. This means that any note played with the first and second valves together can alternately be played third valve.

That small difference between 9½ inches and 10 inches, however, is enough to matter! The note "A" fingered 3 is very low compared to the "A" fingered 1-2. For this reason, third valve is considered a false fingering, and this valve is used only in combination with other valves, except in fast passages when speed is more critical than pitch.

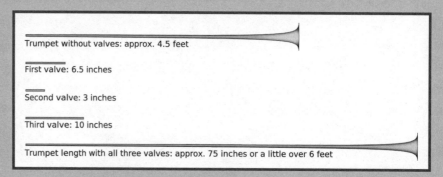

Trumpet without valves: approx. 4.5 feet

First valve: 6.5 inches

Second valve: 3 inches

Third valve: 10 inches

Trumpet length with all three valves: approx. 75 inches or a little over 6 feet

Each valve slide increases the length of the trumpet tubing by a specific amount

The Engine Room

The *valve casing* is the hollow framework into which the valves are inserted. Every pipe on the trumpet is connected at some point to the valve casing, making it the heart and soul of the trumpet! To clean the valve casing, use a cleaning rod with a slit for a soft rag to be inserted (see chapter 17). The casing should be cleaned monthly, since dirt particles will slow your valve action.

Do not use a valve casing brush to clean the casing! In spite of its name, the bristles and metal center of this brush can scratch the inside of the metal casing. Even tiny scratches will cause friction when the valves are pressed.

The three sections of the valve casing are connected by *knuckles*, or hollow jointed tubes, which allow air to flow between the sections (see diagram below). You should clean these knuckles once a month with a soft cloth to remove dirt and deposits, which will otherwise impede the airflow and affect the trumpet's tuning.

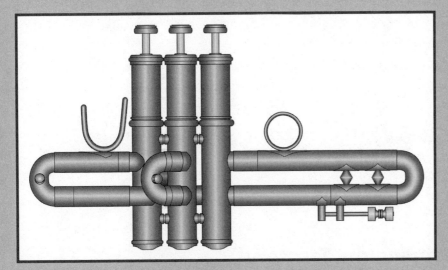

This picture shows the valve casing and valve slides without the leadpipe in front. Between the second and third valve casings, the top and bottom connections are *valve casing bracing points*. The middle connecting point is a *knuckle* that allows air to pass between valve sections. Another knuckle is hidden behind the second valve slide.

Steps and Valves

Valves can be used individually or in combination. The note that is produced is determined by the total length of the trumpet created by the valve or valves.

First Valve Slide—lowers the pitch of the trumpet by two half steps or one full step.

Second Valve Slide—lowers the pitch of the trumpet by one half step.

Third Valve Slide—lowers the pitch of the trumpet by three half steps.

58

The sections of the valve casing are also connected by *valve casing bracing points*. These ball-shaped nodes are attached to the valve sections with *solder* (pronounced "sodder," metal that is melted and then cooled).

Wipe your valve casing after each practice to prevent the sweat and acid from your hands from harming the plating or lacquer.

Down the Tunnel

The inner diameter of a tube is called the *bore*. On a trumpet, the bore is measured not at the leadpipe (the obvious choice), but rather by removing the second valve slide and measuring the inside diameter of the second valve slide.

If you unrolled the trumpet from one end to another, not including the added length of the valve slides, it would be approximately 4.5 feet long. Adding the valve slides increases the length to just over 6 feet—much longer than you might guess from looking!

Mapping the Territory

Although there are various exercises in the back of this book designed to develop specific aspects of your technique, *Buzz to Brilliance* is essentially a handbook, intended to be used alongside one of the several method books available. It offers technique-building exercises from a beginning to an advanced level, marked "Beginner," "Intermediate," and "Advanced," depending on their difficulty. Exercises marked "Cornerstone" are exercises that, once begun, will become an ongoing part of your practice from that point forward. The chapters and exercises within *Buzz to Brilliance* will see you through your first several years of playing, moving you into your advanced training.

Depending on the method book you are using and how much you are practicing, you should be able to complete your first method book in four to nine months. It's natural to want to progress quickly to the harder songs that you really want to play! However, be realistic. If the material you're currently working on is still difficult for you, you're not ready to move on. Give yourself new material only when you can consistently play your current songs with a clear, steady tone, correct fingerings, a steady beat, and good speed.

If you are quickly mastering the songs in your current book—perhaps even playing them accurately the first time you see them—it might be time to ask your band director to recommend additional material for you to practice on

"The most difficult thing is to get the best tone. You can have oodles of technique, but if you've got no tone, it's not going to be attractive to the person hearing it."

— Philip Smith

Your Musical Travel Guide: The Private Teacher

If you know you're interested in developing yourself as a trumpeter, a relationship with a private teacher can be invaluable, both personally and musically. My teachers didn't rise to the top of their field by accident, and their worldly wisdom and advice helped me shape who I wanted to be.

When searching for a teacher, choose someone who has good academic and professional qualifications and a good reputation as a teacher. You want someone who is personable, communicates well, and is willing to explain things until you truly understand them. Performing and teaching are very different skills; just because someone is skilled in one area doesn't mean he or she will be skilled in the other—even if that person is the best trumpeter in town.

Don't choose a particular teacher simply because he or she has the lowest rate. Often—though not always—you will get what you pay for. Getting a "deal" isn't so worthwhile if you progress half as fast!

Take at least two lessons from a teacher before committing to study with that person, and if possible try one or two other teachers to compare. It is harder to leave a teacher once you've established the relationship, so make an informed choice! Invite your parents to participate in this process. Their perspective will give you more information to make your decision.

Two to Tango

A teacher can give you ideas, suggestions, stories, analogies, tricks, and different ways to approach or apply technique. It is up to you to implement these in your own playing. Lessons work only if you practice—both quality and quantity count! Remember that teachers will not ask you to do anything that they have not done themselves.

Your participation in the lesson can make an enormous difference in your relationship with your teacher. Be genuine and open with him or her, come to lessons prepared (and let them know up front when you are not), and come to lessons with an idea of what you want to accomplish. When teachers know a student is interested and motivated, they will give their best time and attention.

Set daily and weekly goals; achieving them will strengthen your motivation. Set long-term goals for yourself and decide how you're going to reach them. You can achieve anything you want, as long as you take action and give it everything you've got!

your own. If you have a private teacher, he or she has probably already taken care of this for you.

The idea is for your material to be challenging enough that it takes you a few days to master each song or exercise. It's nice when things are easy, but it can also get boring. You will get much more out of your experience if you've got challenging music to sink your teeth into.

Now that you have the basics that you need to begin playing, it is time to begin creating a practice routine for yourself. Once you have learned a few songs and exercises, you are ready for the practice routine on page 210, which will allow you to make good progress during your first year of study.

See
Appendix
page 210

60

Breathing

B
reathing is as important to trumpet playing as it is to singing. Besides being essential for your range, volume, and sound quality, your breath is the raw material of your musical lines. It is what will infuse your notes and the rhythms with the expression that you want to create, from a thundering wall of sound to a gently nuanced phrase, and everything in between.

It would seem that correct breathing should come naturally to us, considering how long we've been doing it! However, it's easy to pick up bad habits in our breathing as a result of tension or bad posture. Playing the trumpet requires unlearning some of these habits, in addition to using your lung capacity more efficiently than is called for in everyday life.

Your Diaphragm Doesn't Care

Your *diaphragm* is a sheet of muscle at the bottom of the ribcage, from the *sternum* (in front) to the spine (in back) of your body, just below the lungs. It separates the chest, or thoracic cavity, from the digestive organs in the abdominal cavity (Figure 5.1). The diaphragm is an involuntary muscle; it is controlled by the same part of your brain that keeps your heart beating. The diaphragm receives the signal to move from the *phrenic nerve*—over which you have no direct control. It is only the muscles attached to your rib cage, the *intercostal muscles,* that give you some control over the breathing process.

As we breathe in, the diaphragm descends and the lungs expand downward, creating a vacuum and pulling air into them. As we exhale, the diaphragm retracts, reducing the space inside the lungs and displacing much of the air inside.

FIGURE 5.1

The trunk of the body consists of the lungs in the thoracic cavity, and the digestive organs and other organs in the abdominal cavity, separated by the diaphragm. As the diaphragm expands downward, it moves these organs out of the way so the lungs and rib cage can expand.

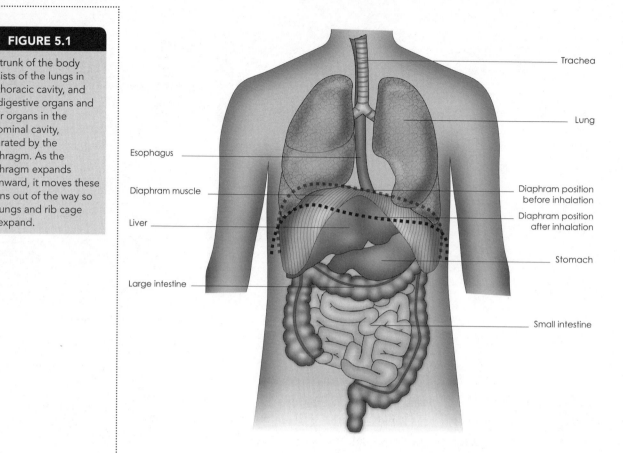

Trachea

Lung

Esophagus

Diaphram muscle

Liver

Large intestine

Diaphram position before inhalation

Diaphram position after inhalation

Stomach

Small intestine

Same Lungs, More Air

The breathing we use in our daily activities doesn't supply enough air to play the trumpet. You might be able to play a note, but it wouldn't last very long! Playing the trumpet relies on expanding your lung capacity and strength, but in a way that is still natural and relaxed.

When you inhale fully, you will notice your breast bone, or sternum, lift slightly. However, an even greater expansion of your breath is actually possible in a place that you've probably never associated with breathing—the lower part of your thoracic cavity, below the sternum but above the intestines, where your floating ribs are located (Figure 5.2). These ribs are attached only at the spine, so more expansion is possible in this area.

If your shoulders rise when you take a breath, you're using the wrong part of your body! Allow the breath to expand upward from the bottom of your chest cavity and into the middle, with your rib cage expanding outward. When you

NOTE: Never take a breath in and hold it! As soon as the breath is taken, release the air and play. If your breathing is tense, your tongue will be more tense (and slower) as well.

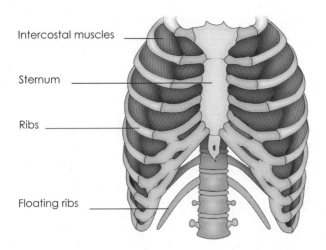

Intercostal muscles

Sternum

Ribs

Floating ribs

FIGURE 5.2

When you breathe, expansion happens in two places—in the lower part of the ribcage, where the floating ribs are located; and in the lifting of the sternum.

63

yawn or sigh, you naturally breathe into this entire area. Take a moment to sigh and notice each of these effects.

When playing, make sure your belt and clothing are loose enough that your whole chest and abdomen can expand freely and comfortably.

Expand the Bellows

Have you ever tried to yell loudly while bending over and touching your toes?

Even if you haven't, you can probably imagine it's a little awkward. You might get a yell out, but it won't be the thundering bellow you're capable of in your finer moments.

In spite of this, plenty of trumpet players try to play with their posture compromised in some way. Your posture directly affects the performance of your diaphragm and breathing! If you are leaning to the side, or tilted too far forward or backward, your lung capacity and movement are reduced.

Gently lift up your sternum to open the rib cage. Hold your head naturally and keep your throat relaxed. Tension in your throat can result in a pinched sound. Some teachers may ask to hear you breathe; however, you are constricting your throat to produce that sound of rushing air.

It is an old myth that you need to use your abdominal muscles to support your breathing. Tensing your abdominal muscles does more than just prevent your chest cavity from expanding; it also automatically causes the back of your throat to close! Clasp your hands together and pull your arms apart to feel this physical reflex, which is called the Valsalva maneuver. When you tense the abdominal muscles and try to breathe, it is sort of like trying to pick up a floor rug while standing on it. Breathe in fully, and save your stomach crunches for some other time.

When you breathe, never imagine that you are pushing and pulling air in either direction, or that you are filling your lungs to capacity. Putting too much thought into physical motions tends to get in the way of naturally performing the movement. Become aware of your posture and sensations, avoid tension, and let your body handle the details.

Take the Nasal Bypass

Whether you're taking the initial breath to play or breathing between phrases of music, you need to breathe through both corners of your mouth. There is more resistance breathing through the nose, so nose breaths are generally not sufficient for trumpet playing.

To breathe through the corners, keep your embouchure on the mouthpiece and loosen only the sides (i.e., the portion of your lips that is still visible when you place your mouthpiece). The opening should be large enough that the breath makes little or no sound. Snap your corners back into your playing embouchure after taking your breath.

If you are a beginning player, it is important to practice breathing this way a few times a day on your mouthpiece so that your lips become familiar with the motion. Alternate breathing and buzzing a few notes, making sure that each note is clear and steady and that your breathing is silent. Once you are comfortable with your breathing, do the same thing on your trumpet.

The only time you will ever breathe through your nose while practicing the trumpet is when you're working on embouchure endurance . . . something we will get to much later in the book.

When Easier Is Better

With all this talk about breathing, you might be tempted to do some pretty weird things as you play. Now is the time to talk about *natural breathing*—which, paraphrased, basically means, "Don't do anything that feels strange, because the uncomfortable things you're doing are probably wrong anyway."

Natural breathing includes taking in only as much air as you need to play a given phrase. To speak the sentence, "Hand me my trumpet," you would not need to inhale to your maximum capacity; your voice is supported and strong even with relatively little inhalation. Likewise, you don't need a full breath to play only three beats.

In general, you should breathe in 25 percent more air than is required to play that passage. By doing this, the passage will be supported by your air "reserves," without your needing to exhale extra air at the end. Likewise, don't pump yourself up like a balloon ready to burst. Your fullest breath should be only 75 percent of your maximum capacity (which you will work on expanding over time). Fifty percent of your full capacity is used to play, while 25 percent supports the sound.

"At golf, tennis, and baseball we work to develop a connection between ourselves and the club, the racquet and the bat. At first, the object is unwieldy and we feel awkward. . . . [with practice] . . . it is as though our hands extend into the object itself.

That oneness, that unison with an object we employ, is the same that we seek to develop with our mouthpiece; it is to become a part of us."

— Rafael Mendez

Two Lungs, a Diaphragm, and a Tuba Player

A gifted tuba player whose career was launched at the age of fifteen with his acceptance to Curtis Institute of Music, Arnold Jacobs stands out in the brass world for his pioneering work in the physiology of breath.

A teacher at Northwestern University and member of the Chicago Symphony for forty-four years, Jacobs' curiosity led him to question the traditional wisdom about breathing. In the process, he discovered that many of the techniques players took for granted were actually harming their playing!

In the following passage, Arnold Jacobs describes the two processes that work together to create a full breath:

65

> The respiratory system . . . should be thought of not as one bellows, but a series of segmented bellows, depending on your posture. When lying on your back on the floor, you will find there is little ability to use chest breathing but you will have a marvelous use of diaphragmatic breathing, which is more than enough to sustain life.
>
> . . .
>
> However, the diaphragm isolated from the rest of the rib cage provides a rather small breath. There is no such thing as a full breath without the use of the sternum. . . . If I lean back on the chair and reach over my head, the motion pulls the rib cage up, which is already in the expanded position. This means I cannot use it for breathing in or out. If I bend forward, pressure in the abdominal region under the diaphragm is such that I have great difficulty using diaphragmatic function.
>
> David Hickman. *Trumpet Pedagogy: A Compendium of Modern Teaching Techniques* (Chandler, Arizona: Hickman Music Editions, 2006), 185.

To discover the principles Jacobs is describing, try out his suggestions:

1. Lie on the floor and place your hands on your belly. Notice how they rise and fall as you breathe.
2. Lean back in your chair and reach over your head. Notice that your rib cage, already lifted, can no longer expand.
3. Hunch forward in your chair. Notice that now your chest can still expand, but your abdominal breathing is limited.

When you breathe correctly, chest and abdominal breathing should happen easily and at the same time. Imagine a deep sigh or a yawn. This is what a full, deep, relaxed breath is meant to feel like!

You can thank Arnold Jacobs for helping you breathe easier at night (see "Two Lungs, a Diaphragm, and a Tuba Player," page 65). This teacher and tuba player rocked the brass world with his penetrating analysis of breathing and its anatomy, dispelling many of the mistakes and myths that players used to swear by.

Breath, with a Side of Stale Air

Now that you know about natural breathing, you can take in the perfect amount of air for each phrase, every single time.

Well, ideally you could. Of course, if playing the trumpet were that simple, you would have been virtuoso two weeks ago. It will take a bit of time to learn exactly how much air you need for each phrase. So . . . what happens if you overshoot and take in too much?

If you do not fully exhale the breath you have just taken in, the excess air from that breath is left in the lungs. Then, when you take in a fresh breath of air, the old, deoxygenated air is still sitting at the bottom of your lungs, taking up room without providing any benefit. You are conserving stale air. This is especially likely to happen when you are nervous and your breathing becomes tense. Eventually, you will be forced to exhale fully so that you can fill your lungs with fresh air.

As you gain experience as a player, you will learn how much to breathe in for each phrase, so that simply playing the phrase uses most of the air you just inhaled. If you end up with excess air and do need to exhale, remove the trumpet from your lips, if possible, to avoid any unexpected honks from your bell.

Except when you're playing the last note of a musical line, air should constantly be moving in or out. Many of us tend to hold our breath, particularly when we're tense. Besides being unhealthy, this constriction compromises your sound when you go to play your next phrase. If you stay relaxed while you play, your breathing will tend to be full and relaxed as well.

Blowing Out the Candle

You may remember from earlier in the chapter that the intercostal muscles surrounding the rib cage help expand and contract the chest cavity. When you sigh, you naturally expel air until these muscles reach their resting state. It is possible to exhale even further by consciously using these muscles to compress the lung cavity.

When you play, the intercostal muscles perform a critical function: besides allowing you to exhale more air, they also allow you to push the air out faster. To blow fast air (essential for good breath support on the trumpet), you will rapidly contract your intercostal muscles.

"Without air or wind there is no tone."

— Hebert L. Clarke

66

The air you use to play the trumpet is just like the air you use to blow out a candle: fast and controlled. If your sound is cracking or you are not achieving the desired notes, try using faster air!

Work Those Intercostals

For a simple breathing exercise you can practice anywhere, place a piece of paper against the wall. Now blow fast air and see how long you can hold it there! Keep good posture throughout the exercise.

Turn to page 216 for some additional breathing exercises that will allow you to independently develop this aspect of your playing.

When you are playing the trumpet, it is difficult to notice your breathing because there are so many other things to pay attention to! By spending part of each practice concentrating on your breathing alone, you can really start to understand this element of brass playing. If you practice proper breathing on a regular basis, you will begin to notice increased endurance and a fuller sound in your playing.

See exercise page 216

67

Articulation

For my fourteenth birthday, I got a cassette tape of Wynton Marsalis called *Carnival*. The entire recording was cornet solos, and that cornet did not stand a chance against Wynton! He executed huge leaps at dizzying speeds, and played short, staccato notes so fast it sounded like a machine gun.

He made it sound easy, but I had played long enough to know that it wasn't.

"Articulation" is the term used to describe the beginnings and endings of notes. Just as in speaking, your articulation communicates the mood and energy of a piece. It was not just speed that made Wynton's solos brilliant. It was their crisp clarity, their sizzling precision and incisive leading edge that grabbed your attention, woke you up.

As in painting, the edges of your notes can be clear and well defined, or they may have a softer edge. Do you want a crisp, bold sound, like a pen-and-ink drawing? Do you want a softer, gentler mood, like a watercolor with gentle blends? As you gain sophistication as a musician, you will consciously choose different articulation styles for different musical passages. The first step to developing those nuances, though, is the ability to maintain exact consistency and precision in whatever articulation you choose.

Flick of the Tongue

The trumpet sound should almost always have a very distinct beginning and end. You will most often use the syllable "too" to begin each note. This hard consonant gives a clear, concise articulation. When you speak the word "too," your tongue is interrupting and then releasing the air, giving the note a crisp beginning as though striking a bell with a mallet. Think of your air like water running out of a kitchen faucet. Imagine moving your index finger through the water in a quick slicing motion, disturbing the water flow as little as possible. Your tongue is like your finger; it flicks across the airflow, causing a brief interruption but without affecting the source of the air.

To create the "too" articulation, the tip of your tongue should strike the hard palate, or *alveolar ridge* (Figure 6.1), which is basically the roof of your mouth, in the front. Be sure the tongue never touches the back of the teeth or passes through the lips! After releasing the "t" in "too," your tongue will be floating in its resting position, the "oo" vowel, which is used for notes in the middle range of the trumpet.

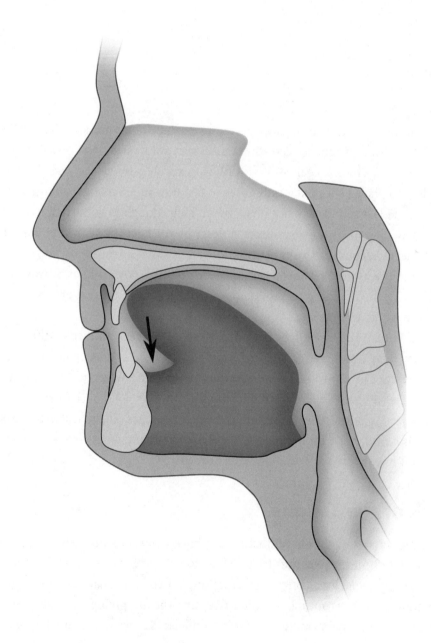

FIGURE 6.1

Tongue position for the "too" syllable. The tip of the tongue should touch the roof of the mouth just behind the teeth, on the alveolar ridge.

Single-Tongue, Unleashed

When you use only the "too" syllable for your articulation, the technique is called "single-tonguing"—single, because you are using only one consonant (the "t" sound). For extremely fast-tongued passages we have another technique waiting for you: multiple-tonguing. You'll learn this technique only in your second or third year of playing, so we'll save it for a little later in the chapter. The path to Wynton-like brilliance is a clear, precise single-tongue technique, so spare nothing in developing the accuracy, precision and speed of your single-tongue!

Try pronouncing "too too too too" out loud, keeping a seamless, steady sound and using the very tip of your tongue for the "t" sound. Keep the air flow constant—the tongue simply intersects the airflow to create the articulation at the beginning of the note. Imagine that your breath is pushing the tongue out of the way each time you articulate "too."

Once you have achieved a high level of consistency, try the same thing on the mouthpiece, on a single note. Make sure that your tongue strikes the hard palate each time, and keep a steady rhythm. The sound should not stutter or burst—you want clear, even notes, each one identical to the next.

As you speak these syllables, keep a close watch on the vowel! The pure "too" and "koo" syllables will facilitate a quicker double- and triple-tongue than "tuh" and "kuh" (with the short "u" sound used in "duck") that you might fall into if you're not paying attention. The "too" is pronounced with the back of the tongue relatively higher in the mouth than for "tuh," leading to a smoother, more efficient articulation.

Tongue Meets Trumpet

After practicing tonguing on your mouthpiece, do the same thing on your trumpet, again on a single note. Practice articulating "too" on middle G (fingered open). Once you have a good grasp of tonguing the G, move to F (fingered first valve). Finally, continue to the remaining notes in the middle range of the trumpet. As you begin to get comfortable with the basic tongue stroke, try "Articulation Acceleration" (page 232), a daily exercise that, over time, will develop your lightning-fast tongue.

See exercise page 232

Once you can accurately articulate these individual notes, you are ready to coordinate your tongue strikes with valve (fingering) changes. Start by alternating between middle F and middle G, making sure each tongue strike happens at exactly the same moment you press or release the valve. Next, choose other pairs of notes and practice alternating between them, always keeping tongue and fingers perfectly synchronized. When you are ready, challenge yourself with "Tongue and Finger Coordination" (page 244).

See exercise page 244

After you've been playing a few months, you will begin to play notes in the lower range of the trumpet. This includes anything from the C below the staff and lower. The "oh" tongue position of the lower range will become "toh" when you are tonguing. The tip of your tongue will still strike the hard palate, but the body of the tongue will be lower.

As you can now guess, the higher notes (G just above the staff and higher) will use the "tee" syllable.

Having the Last Note

We usually think of articulation in reference to note beginnings, but articulation is all about the place where two notes meet. This means it's also about note endings.

In general, your tongue flick takes care of both the end of one note and the beginning of the next. The exception to this is the last note of a phrase, where, perhaps counter to your instinct, you should not use your tongue. The abrupt "thud" you'll hear when you plug up the dam with your tongue should be a good reminder that this is not the way to go.

To release the last note of a musical line in your songs, or for longer pauses within musical lines, just stop your exhale. Don't use your tongue, and be sure you're not closing the back of your throat, either—just stop the breath. Later you'll learn to slightly taper the note to gracefully end your musical phrase.

At the end of a line of music, wait a full second and then remove your trumpet. This allows the embouchure to finish vibrating and the sound to ring inside your bell.

Common Articulation Problems

Speed: To increase your speed, consistently practice articulation drills, challenging yourself daily to increase your speed. Move to a faster speed only when your tonguing at the slower tempo is nearly perfect. If you push yourself too quickly, you will have to backtrack later, so you are not moving any faster in the long run.

Jaw Movement: There is no reason for your jaw to move if you are articulating correctly. Too much jaw movement will result in a less distinct articulation, undesirable variation in your tone, and reduced note accuracy. Clip a mirror to your stand when you practice to stay aware of your embouchure.

Coordination: Some articulation problems actually arise from a lack of coordination between the tongue and the fingers of the right hand. The tongue must strike at precisely the same time the valve is fully pressed or released. If you discover that your tongue and fingers are working at cross purposes, practice the troublesome pattern slowly, increasing your speed once you have achieved accuracy at the slower speed.

One Line, Many Notes

Articulation is about the stuff that happens between two notes. In some cases, that stuff is absolutely nothing! Your tongue is momentarily off duty—at least as far as articulation is concerned.

Whenever you move between notes without tonguing, you are playing a slur—a musical term for notes played smoothly, one to the next. Slurs are found in many types of music—even fanfares! You will find them both in beautiful, lyrical passages and in music that is so rapid that there is no need to tongue. Listen to Rimsky Korsakov's "Flight of the Bumble Bee," performed by Wynton Marsalis, for an example of the latter.

Violinists create slurs by playing several notes on the same bow direction, rather than changing bow direction with each note. Pianists create the same effect by using a fluid wrist motion to glide through the notes, overlapping them slightly to create a seamless line. Wind players (including brass players) slur by changing from one note to the next without tonguing. The marking for all of these slurs is the same—a curved line that arches over two or more notes in the printed music.

There are two types of slurs on a brass instrument. In a lip slur, you are changing notes simply by tightening and loosening the embouchure (your tongue will, of course, rise and fall as needed). To achieve smooth, clear lip slurs, you will need to loosen or tighten your embouchure a precise amount in one single, swift moment. The other type of slur is a valve slur; you will similarly need to press or release the valve(s) in one quick motion. For both lip

Your Many-Talented Tongue

Here are the various articulations you can produce using your tongue.

Tongued Articulation—tongue strike, using "too," "koo," or another syllable

Slur—The tongue may articulate the first note of a slur, but notes under the slur are not articulated.

Lip Slur—A lip slur refers to two consecutive notes played on the same valve by changing the aperture and tongue height.

Legato Tongue—The tongue executes a gentle articulation, leading to a smooth, connected sound that is still tongued.

Staccato Tongue—The tongue strikes and returns to its resting position very rapidly, resulting in notes that are extremely short and separated.

FIGURE 6.2

The top scale above is tongued, while the scale below is played slurred (played without tongue strikes between notes).

74

See exercise page 225

slurs and valve slurs, you may begin the passage with a "too" articulation, but the notes that follow are smooth and connected, with no additional tongue strikes.

Both valve slurs and lip slurs will require individual attention as you encounter them in your music . . . no less than tongued passages! Facility with lip slurs in particular is an entire discipline within trumpet playing, and is part of developing very fine control over your embouchure.

Figure 6.2 shows an example of the same five-note scale written tongued and slurred. For the notes in the second example, each of the note changes is a valve slur.

During your first year of playing, you will encounter many valve slurs, and occasional lip slurs as well. You will find exercises and detailed instructions for developing your lip slurs on page 225. Start with the easier ones and slowly work your way down the page. By the end of your first year of study you should be working on some of the harder lip slur exercises.

Multiple-Tonguing

In salsa dancing, it all starts with the basic step. Quick, quick, slow. Quick, quick, slow.

The spiraling dance patterns that are created around this framework are pure art in motion—but those fundamental steps must be perfectly balanced, effortless, and immaculately synchronized to the music, or the more sophisticated patterns quickly become a disorganized mess.

Likewise, your single-tongue is the foundation of your tonguing technique. It is used when the notes occur slowly enough that the tip of the tongue has time to return to the hard palate for each new note; and it must be perfectly even, rhythmic, and impeccable. Your "too" syllable, used alone, will always give you the most consistent articulation.

Somewhere around the beginning of your second year of study, though, you will begin to encounter occasions when the notes are too fast to articulate "too" each time. At these faster speeds, you will add a different syllable, "koo," so that you are alternately interrupting the airflow with the tip and middle of the tongue, gaining additional speed. You should still use single-tonguing whenever possible; only multiple-tongue when it is impossible to single-tongue.

See exercise page 238

As you begin your foray into multiple-tonguing, you will learn triple-tonguing first, which combines the syllables "too" and "koo" in a three-note pattern, "too too koo." Use simple songs as a springboard into linguistic brilliance, starting with "Articulation Variations" (page 238). Once you are secure in your triple-tonguing, you will drop one of the "too" syllables, creating the double-tongue pattern. Triple-tonguing is actually easier than double-tonguing because it doesn't require you to switch between "too" and "koo" on every single note.

Catching Up Your Koo

As with single-tonguing, you will need to practice multiple-tonguing slowly and carefully so that you have good control at every speed. You will notice that "koo" is a weaker syllable, simply because you've been using "too" for a year already! To improve your "koo" articulation, first practice saying "koo koo koo koo koo," then practice this articulation on your mouthpiece alone. Once you move to the trumpet, spend a week or two playing familiar songs using only "koo." Your goal is to make your "koo" as clear and consistent as your "too."

Once you are comfortable with the "koo" articulation, practice the "too too koo" (triple-tonguing) pattern, first spoken and then on your mouthpiece. Place the "koo" articulation as close to the front of the mouth as possible (Figure 6.3)—but without placing it so far forward that the sides of the tongue lock against the teeth. Placing the "koo" relatively forward in the mouth makes the "koo" sound more similar to "too," and will also allow you to articulate more quickly. You will also be faster if you keep your tongue strike relatively light.

Gradually increase the speed of your tonguing on the mouthpiece; you are ready to play faster only when every note is perfectly clear and accurate. When you are comfortable, try the same thing on the trumpet, gradually increasing your speed. Try the pattern at a soft then a loud dynamic, since the tongue will react slightly differently to the different intensity of air.

Ping-Pong for the Tongue

When you are experienced with triple-tonguing, you are ready to move to the last step, which is double-tonguing. You will take the "too too koo" pattern and simply drop a "too," so that you are now rapidly alternating "too koo." You will notice that learning double-tonguing is a little easier than learning triple-tonguing was, because you have already begun to master the new syllable "koo."

If your "too" and "koo" sounds are quite different, this will become very apparent when you double-tongue, because there is no "too too" repetition to smooth the effect! Listen closely to your note beginnings to make these syllables nearly identical. Also, remember, the accuracy and clarity of your multiple-tongue is a reflection of your single-tonguing skill on each syllable.

"The attack should be started as distinctly as possible and must be positive. But there is a difference in using the tongue when playing loud or soft, also when playing either high or low registers."

— Herbert L. Clarke

75

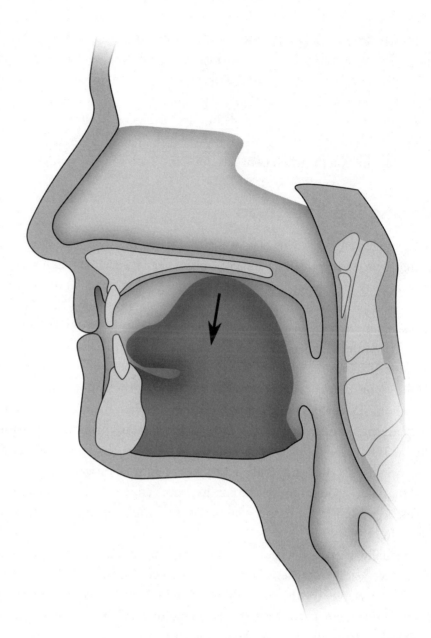

FIGURE 6.3

Tongue position for the "koo" syllable. The middle of the tongue, which articulates the "koo," should be as close to the front of the mouth as possible.

"The compression of air behind the tongue at impact determines the sharpness of the attack."

— Roger Bobo

If your tongue is slow, don't expect any miracles; get your "too" up to speed! Your tongue is a muscle, and you are training it like any other muscle in your body. Use the exercises on the next page, "Gymnastics for Your Tongue," to get your tongue in shape. Leave behind your concerns about practice time; your tongue is always with you!

Articulating Excellence

As you advance on the trumpet, other articulations can be added to the basic "too" and "koo," to create a particular musical gesture. "Your Many-Talented Tongue" (page 73) lists the various styles of articulation that are possible with the techniques covered so far.

Gymnastics for Your Tongue

Triple-tongue Syllable Combinations

Koo Koo Koo   Koo Koo Koo (etc.—strengthen your "koo" alone)

Too Too Koo   Too Too Koo   Too Too Koo   Too Too Koo

Too Koo Too   Koo Too Koo   Too Koo Too   Koo Too Koo

Double-tongue Syllable Combinations

Too Koo Too Koo   Too Koo Too Koo   Too Koo Too Koo   Too Koo Too Koo

Too Too Too Too   Koo Koo Koo Koo   Too Too Too Too   Koo Koo Koo Koo

Too Koo Koo Too   Koo Too Too Koo   Too Koo Koo Too   Koo Too Too Koo

Designed for you to practice your tonguing, these exercises are genuine tongue twisters. Don't miss a chance to walk down the hall to your next class and improve your articulation at the same time!

When you are ready, some new syllables can be brought into play for a more legato articulation or in softer playing. "Doo," "loo," and "goo" will all create a more gentle, indistinct note beginning. You'll still want to use "too" for clarity in most situations; the alternate syllables can cause your note to sound late in phrases where a clear, crisp start is needed.

If you are having trouble eliminating an aggressive or heavy initial articulation in a quiet passage, try "poo" as an alternative. This is called a "breath attack," in which the very fast air causes the lips to burst apart. Ironically, even though the air is very fast, the breath attack lends a more subtle beginning to the note. As with other alternate articulations, breath atacks are a great option for certain entrances, but if you use them too often, they will become an idiosyncrasy of your playing, losing their individual distinction and nuance.

If you really wanted to, you could get by with average articulation. Plenty of players do. However, Wynton Marsalis did not sell five million CDs by just getting by. Developing excellent articulation isn't that difficult, and you'll be impressed with yourself once you start getting results!

Warm-Up and Warm-Down

Chris struggled through the first two lines of his region band solo. He had transferred from another school in the middle of the year, so we'd been working together for about a month.

"This passage has sounded about the same for a couple weeks now. How much have you been practicing?" I asked. He was a responsible kid, and I knew that he took pride in his playing.

"Twenty minutes, sometimes thirty," he answered.

"Twenty minutes? That's just enough time to remember where your lips are and find a few notes that you forgot since your last practice!" Chris looked at me with surprise.

It turns out that until that conversation, Chris's practicing had always been a pretty unstructured time: play this week's band material, give the hard songs an extra two or three tries, then go back to his old favorites from last year. He thought of practice kind of like, "Time to relax and hang out with my trumpet," as opposed to, "Time to make something happen!" No one becomes a marathon-level runner by jogging around the block every day. Similarly, Chris's current practicing was just barely enough to get him warmed up before he turned around and put the trumpet back in the case.

While it is important to practice long enough, it is equally important to practice smart and develop good physical and mental habits. This chapter focuses on ways to keep yourself physically healthy by toning and conditioning your muscles before and after your practice. Some material in this chapter is oriented more toward intermediate or advanced players; if you are a beginning player, return to the chapter every so often as your playing advances and you are ready to add additional exercises.

Wake-Up Call

Your warm-up should be the first thing you do when you unpack your trumpet for the first time each day. The goal of a warm-up is to loosen the lips before practice; just as a runner would never run without stretching their muscles first, so should a trumpeter always warm-up before playing. The warm-up gets you mentally and physically in gear, toning your body and waking up your mind!

Your warm-up will serve as an alert if your concentration, coordination or focus is lacking, so that you can get in the right mental space. It will also let you know where your technique stands on a daily basis.

Yoga for Your Lips

A good warm-up consists of a minimum of five minutes for beginning players, or a more extensive ten- to fifteen-minute warm-up for more advanced players. Your warm-up is designed to loosen up your muscles, not work them out; so relax and enjoy this part of your practice! If you are tired after your warm-up, make it a little shorter.

The length of your warm-up should correspond to the length of your total practice. If you are an advanced player, your warm-up will be longer. Rest two to five minutes between warm-up exercises, especially in the morning when your lips are puffy from sleep. See the sample warm-up routine on the next page for an idea of how to design a warm-up routine that suits your needs.

If you are serious about your playing, you should do two or three thirty-minute practice sessions daily (including warm-up time) beginning in your second year of study. It is not necessary to do an extensive warm-up for your second and third sessions each day, since your embouchure should be fairly limber after the first session. Warming up more than you need at this point will take valuable practice time that could be used for music and etudes.

Ten Minutes, Twenty Options

See exercises pages 253, 232

See exercise page 245

Use the warm-up to break in skills you will need later in your playing session, including flexibility, range, key of the piece, multiple articulations, and specific technical skills. For example, if you need to play a high G in your rehearsal, then your warm-up also needs to incorporate this note.

Your warm-up time is a perfect opportunity to review scales (see page 253) and articulation studies (page 232). In addition, you will hear Stamp's Warm-Up (page 245) anywhere you find a trumpeter, from the band hall to

Sample Warm-up Routine

The warm-ups below use books listed on page 91. Beginning players should play only the exercises marked with an asterisk.

* 1. Buzz sirens and long tones on your mouthpiece alone
* 2. Play long tones on the trumpet; Schlossberg Daily
     Drills #1–2 is a good routine

REST

3. Intonation Drills
4. James Stamp Studies #3
* 5. Arban pages 42–43, for flexibility

REST

6. Clark Technical Studies #2, for finger dexterity, slurred
7. Same as above, but this time tongued
8. Double- and triple-tonguing exercises from Arban, and on major and minor scales

REST

9. Extreme register drills: warm up the highest and lowest notes you will need to play this session
10. Lyrical playing, to get you listening musically

REST means 2–5 minutes without playing, to let your lips recover.

backstage at major symphony orchestras. Choose your warm-up routine thoughtfully and change routines every so often. Give this time your best-quality concentration to set yourself up for a powerful practice session!

Pamper Your Pucker

As much as you want to use your practice time efficiently, it is equally important to rest your lips. This will give your lips a chance to recover the proper blood supply and be ready to play again. Practicing consistently with small breaks will help you build muscle strength and stamina.

If your practice time is limited on a given day, you can help keep your lips toned by buzzing on your mouthpiece during down time, such as during homework or traveling in the car. Always use the proper technique so that you condition the correct muscles.

Practicing with a friend is a great way to make use of your practice time. When you and your friend get together to practice trumpet, chances are you will occasionally stop to talk about the music, play for each other, and even listen to recordings. This means you're resting about as much as you are playing, which creates a good balance. If you play your music together, you will also be developing good listening and ensemble skills.

A Good Rub-Down

Your warm-down is designed to provide a gentle massage for your lips after a practice or performance. The warm-down gets blood flowing back into the lips and massages the freshly exercised muscles in the embouchure.

Without a proper warm-down, your embouchure muscles may be sore or tighter than usual the next day. This will require extra warm-up time that you may or may not have! If you do multiple practice sessions each day, do a complete warm-down after each one.

During the warm-down, avoid any note above third-space C and play at a soft dynamic, exerting very little pressure on the lips. Here are some specific warm-down activities:

See exercise page 221

- Play long tones in the low register ("Long Tones," page 221, exercises 2–3) with little mouthpiece pressure.
- Using light mouthpiece pressure, play notes in the low register of the trumpet (see Figure 7.1) in quarter, eighth and sixteenth note patterns.
- Use your fingertips to gently massage your embouchure muscles in a circular motion for twenty to thirty seconds.
- After a particularly strenuous workout, place a warm cloth on your face to gently loosen and relax the muscles.

82

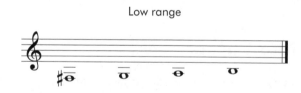

Low range

Middle range

High range

FIGURE 7.1

Low, middle and high range of the trumpet. Your high range will vary depending on your level of advancement (see Figure 9.2, page 99).

Building Chops to Last

As you do your warm-up and warm-down, make sure the corners of the embouchure remain anchored (firm and locked in one position). Firmly closed corners will create a seal that prevents air from escaping while you play. This ensures that your wind will actually make it into your sound—a much more efficient way to play!

Most endurance and strength problems in trumpet playing are the result of weak corners. Use long tones, lip bends, and lip flexibilities listed in the exercises section to build strength in the facial muscles that create firm corners. Keeping good breath support will also help keep your embouchure from working harder than it needs to.

Not for the Faint of Lip

As you have begun to discover, your lips lose blood flow (and oxygen) while the mouthpiece is placed on them—even with relatively little pressure! If you've ever had a bad sunburn, you might have noticed that when you press your finger on your skin for several seconds then take it away, it leaves a white circle where your finger pad was. Those few seconds were enough time for your finger pressure to push the blood out.

If you keep your mouthpiece on your lips too long, the reduced circulation will eventually create fatigue, and your lips will stop responding. Reducing your mouthpiece pressure will improve your endurance, but you still need to rest frequently to allow blood to return to your lips. Lip flapping is a quick way to get blood circulating in your lips again (see page 49).

In performance, take the mouthpiece off your lips as often as possible during the rests. A little bit of rest goes a long way!

They're Not Made of Steel

Performance injuries often result from a dramatic increase in playing time without conditioning your muscles first. It is not uncommon for trumpeters to bruise their lips with too much practice or insufficient rest. Minor bruising can be painful and require a few days off to recover, while more serious bruising can result in sensitive nerves and even blood vessel damage. When building your technique, always increase your playing time gradually.

If your lips are fatigued from lots of playing—for example, during a heavy rehearsal schedule or band camp—it is important to rest and restore them as soon as possible. If the concert is still ahead and you must continue playing, minimize your mouthpiece pressure, don't play unless you have to, and take the mouthpiece off your lips at every opportunity!

Once your demanding schedule is over, it is time to take care of your muscles. Normal playing won't give them a chance to recover, but don't stop playing altogether, either! If you suddenly take time off, your overworked muscles will become stiff. Focus on light playing, resting more frequently than usual. Gradually increase your practice to its usual intensity over a period of several days.

Practice: Laying the Foundation

Practice.

What can I say, other than, "Everybody has to do it!"?

Although practice can be fun when you're seeing great results, there will always be those days when you would rather leave the trumpet in the case and head to the lake. Wouldn't it be great to simply pick up the trumpet and be able to play anything you wanted to?

In reality, though, practice is what it takes to get results in almost anything in life, and playing the trumpet is no exception.

There are ways to cut down on the number of hours you spend in the practice room, though. If you "practice smart," you can learn material more quickly and avoid lapsing into bad habits that will ultimately slow you down. The "brute force" approach solves every problem with the same solution: "You just need to practice more!" If you use effective practice techniques, though, you can become a brilliant player and still have your day at the lake.

Set Daily Goals

Whether it is playing a line of music up to speed or playing your song flawlessly, daily goals give your practice focus and direction.

Before each practice session write down what you want to accomplish. This will ensure that you are spending your time where it counts the most.

"Would a weightlifting student, because they were able to lift their first light barbell, immediately go on to a heavier one?

Of course not; they would have to develop so much on their first one. And you are the same."

— Rafael Mendez

86

Laurence Peter, the famous writer and thinker, once said, "If you don't know where you're going, you'll probably end up somewhere else!"

Before you start your practice each day, finish any immediate tasks you need to complete so that nothing is pulling at your attention, and set up your practice area so that you don't have any distractions in your physical space. Mark your trouble spots during each rehearsal so that you can easily find them when you practice. Develop a practice routine that gives you time to develop each element of your playing, and know when you have achieved each of your goals for the day.

With concrete goals as your benchmark, it is easy to know if your practicing is getting you somewhere! Clear goals also give you the freedom to walk away from your practicing when you've met your goal. Sometimes it is satisfying to practice until you are fatigued, but the important thing is the result.

Practice Badly, Play Badly

There are as many ideas for "practicing smart" as there are creative players to develop them. However, the foundation for all good practicing is reinforcing good technique and avoiding repeating your mistakes.

The more you practice a passage incorrectly, the more you're programming yourself to play the incorrect pattern. This is going to double the work you have to put in! First you have to unlearn the incorrect pattern, then you have to learn what you missed the first time. This applies equally to wrong notes, rhythms, and sloppy articulation.

Like athletes, musicians create lasting imprints in our physical memory through practice, strengthening particular nervous system pathways each time

Accuracy in Your Practice

Long hours of practice translate into flawless technique only if at the end of your practice session you are better than when you started! Useful practice strategies allow you to reduce errors each time you play a passage, rather than reinforcing errors by repeating them.

As you are practicing, notice problem areas and work on them separately, measure by measure. If there is a particular note you are missing, practice getting to that note from the one before. Gradually add notes on both sides, until the measure is flawless and reliable.

After spending time on this detail work, play the etude or piece all the way through, trying not to make any mistakes. Don't stop and go back; instead, continue to the end. Review any trouble spots, then repeat, again without stopping to correct mistakes.

we perform a particular movement. If you practice badly, you will perform badly. If you practice passages incorrectly, you will perform them incorrectly.

If you're practicing a lot without making very much progress, see if you can figure out other ways to practice the trouble spots, and ask your teacher for better practice strategies. Our mistakes and habits aren't accidents—we've carefully practiced every single one!

One Bite at a Time

There is something incredibly rewarding about playing through a whole song without stopping. You have a sense of accomplishment at the end, like working for hours on a jigsaw puzzle so you can have the satisfaction of putting in that very last piece. We tend to think of it like running a race—the important thing is to make it to the finish line!

However, *practicing* and *playing* are not the same thing at all. If you only play your songs from beginning to end, the hard parts are never going to get easier because you're spending so much time playing the whole thing! Besides that, by the time you get to the end of the song, you have forgotten the mistakes at the beginning that you wanted to fix.

Break your songs up into manageable pieces as you practice. Spend your time on the hardest parts, and make sure the end gets just as much attention as the beginning. If you are going to do a run-through, do it at the beginning so you know what to work on, and another at the end so you can see what you've accomplished.

Don't Tune Yourself Out

We often stop listening to ourselves when we're practicing and instead get caught up in other issues such as notes, fingerings, or that story someone told us at lunch today. Stop! Get back on track and listen to what you're doing.

Have in mind what you want to sound like while you are practicing. Routines, while they have their place, should be used with caution—the repetition can cause you to stop listening. Don't just play through something to play through it! Improve upon some aspect every time you play a passage.

In the heat of the moment, it's easy to forget to slow down and work through a difficult passage. We get so wrapped up in the excitement (or anxiety) of playing a difficult passage that we forget to practice intelligently. However, slow practice is crucial to a good performance.

If you take the time to slow the passage down and work through it, you will gradually reinforce the correct way to play it. Then you're ready to gradually increase the speed. Never go faster than you are able to play well.

Often we will find ourselves making the same mistakes over and over again, even when we know how to fix them. This isn't a technique issue; it's a

"Practice, practice, practice until it all works correctly— by habit."

— Claude Gordon

87

"It is important to practice often during the day, and not a long time. Play thirty minutes, and rest fifteen minutes. Then play thirty minutes, rest thirty minutes. Play thirty minutes and rest an hour. The lips are a muscle and it is important to rest them frequently. . . ."

— Maurice Andre

Four Tools to Advance Your Playing

Metronome

A metronome is kind of a musical lie detector. While it's easy to get annoyed when it tells us things we'd rather not know, it is like a good friend—it tells us what we most need to know!

Use a metronome for up to 80 percent of your practicing, both to keep your tempo steady and to increase your speed to the final tempo. Over time, practicing with a metronome creates an internal pulse that will stay with you even when the metronome is off.

Tuner

As you know, there are many notes on the trumpet that are noticeably flat or sharp. Take the time to learn the tendencies of your own instrument. You may be surprised that certain notes you were taking for granted are way off! Play your songs slowly with a tuner to check your accuracy, and review familiar material to make sure you're still on target.

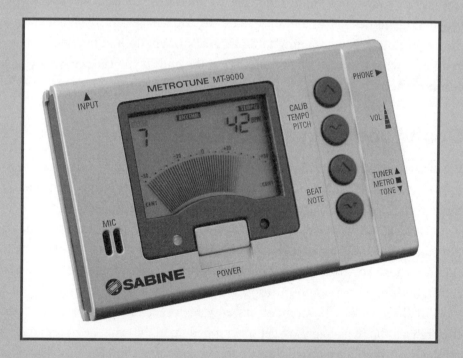

Turn off your tuner while playing with an ensemble, unless you are slowly working through a particular section as a group. With many players and many different instruments, you will need to adjust your tuning to the ensemble around you.

Recording Device

Recording your practice sessions is a great way for both students and professionals to improve their playing. It is easy to get used to the way you sound and forget to listen with fresh ears! Review your recorded sessions after you practice to get a true sense of your strengths and gaps.

There are many affordable handheld devices on the market. Stay away from those that are primarily voice recorders; these devices are designed for people who need to take notes from a conversation, and cannot handle the wide range of pitch and volume in music. You may find the best recording quality using your home computer or laptop, once equipped with inexpensive (or free) recording software and a good microphone. A laptop is also great for recording when you are away from home.

Listen to your recorded sessions carefully and honestly. You must be your own toughest critic. If you don't find your own weaknesses, someone else will!

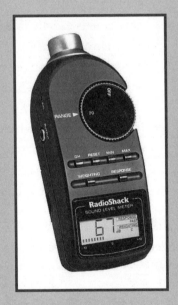

Decibel Meter

As we concentrate on simply getting the notes out with a good sound, we often unintentionally fluctuate between loud and soft in musical passages. If you are beginning to work on advanced literature, consider downloading a decibel meter app for your smartphone or other mobile device, or borrow a decibel meter from your teacher.

concentration issue. When you can play something correctly and you don't, ask yourself where your attention was. Was it on playing that thing correctly? Often our attention wanders and we don't even realize it until the measure has come and gone.

Many mistakes will disappear as soon as you genuinely decide to stop making them. Just before you reach the make-or-break moment, remind yourself of the note or technique you're going to perform instead. With your attention on the right thing at the right time, you will discover that passages that tripped you up for weeks are not as difficult as they seem.

See
exercise
page 219

See
exercise
page 218

Metronome Practice

To an advancing student such as yourself, it may seem like a great idea to skip rhythm practice so you can spend more time on your lesson or band material. However, you will often spend extra time struggling with the same rhythmic patterns in your music that you didn't master with the metronome!

Work with the metronome drills on page 219, or choose a few measures of your band or orchestra music to get your "metronome chops" for the day. Here are a few suggestions:

- Choose a slow tempo, around 60 beats per minute (bpm). Increase the tempo by two to four bpm once you can accurately play your current tempo.
- Know when the next click is about to happen, and make sure your next note is exactly lined up with it.
- The metronome should be reinforcing your own sense of beat, not replacing it. As you're practicing, try to line up your internal beat with the beat you're hearing. Then, when you finally turn off the click, don't turn off your inner metronome!
- If you are not sure what notes should line up with the click, sit down with the music and a pencil and figure out where the beats are. Mark each beat with a diagonal slash. Then practice speaking the rhythm out loud using the syllables on page 218.

Turn your metronome on frequently during your practice. It will help keep you focused and improve your rhythmic precision.

Rough and Ragged, with Purpose

It is very tempting to play the pieces you are good at and avoid the pieces that look hard! Playing those easy pieces gives you a great sense of accomplishment. However, if you practice only what you sound good on, you are going to be the same player a year from now that you are right now.

It is important to give yourself permission to make mistakes and work on the hard, messy spots. Don't be self-conscious about who's listening, or feel like you need to sound good all the time—it is more important to work on the stuff you *can't* do! When you do hear something that sounds bad, don't move on to the next spot without addressing the problem.

Every practice session should focus on at least one weakness in your playing. In time and with practice, you can change what you can't do to what you can do.

Essential Studies for Intermediate Trumpet

Arban, J. B. *Complete Conservatory Method*. New York: Carl Fischer, 1981.

With 380 pages of non-stop trumpet technique, the book is a must for your trumpet library. It covers all areas of trumpet technique, and includes duets and cornet solos.

Clarke, H. L. *Technical Studies*. New York: Carl Fischer, 1934.

This book will get you working on endurance, range, breath control, flexibility, and finger speed in all keys.

Schlossberg, M. *Daily Drills and Technical Studies*. New York: M. Baron Company, 1941.

With exercises for breathing, long tones, articulation, flexibility, arpeggios, and scales, this book is a daily workout to help you improve the fundamentals of your playing.

Stamp, J. *Warm-Ups & Studies*. Bulle, Switzerland: Editions BIM, 1978.

In addition to the warm-ups used by every trumpet professional, this book features exercises for lip buzzing, mouthpiece buzzing, pedal tones, breath control, lip bends, slurs, trills, and articulation.

Mouthpiece Medicine

Mouthpiece buzzing is ideal for practicing any passage in which you are having difficulty getting your embouchure position to the correct notes. If you're playing a passage and you keep missing a particular leap, practice glissing (sliding the pitch) between the two notes using the mouthpiece alone. Then practice alternating between the notes without the glissando, consciously imagining each pitch just before you play it. This repetition will help establish muscle memory for the notes.

Buzzing is also an effective troubleshooting technique any time your note beginnings are fuzzy or unresponsive. Play the first note of the melody on your trumpet to get a starting pitch, then remove the mouthpiece and buzz the whole melody on your mouthpiece. Listen to the buzz quality of each note. Your goal should be a strong, steady, resonant note with a clean, clear beginning. Make sure your sound is steady and consistent, then return to the trumpet.

"Don't practice quickly and hope it gets better. Practice excellence and hope it gets faster."

— Frank Gabriel Campos

How Much Time Should I Practice for Band?

Your band or orchestra music is designed with everyone in mind. You will have fun playing this music, but it's almost always going to be easier than your private-lesson assignments. It is the technical studies and repertoire from your private lessons that will push you to your limit as a player, allowing you to learn your band and orchestra music more quickly as well!

For this reason, you should concentrate your practice sessions on your private-lesson material, spending about two-thirds of your playing time on it.

Difficult passages may occasionally arise in your band or orchestra music, requiring a larger portion of your practice time to "woodshed" a new part. However, make sure you reserve time for your lesson material even on these days, and learn the ensemble part as efficiently as possible.

If you discover that you are spending too much time on your band or orchestra music during your practice sessions, bring the difficult passages to your lesson. Your teacher should be able to clear up any technical or musical difficulties and may assign you some specific exercises that address that technical concern. This will build your technique in that area, while also improving the ensemble piece.

The bottom line is, when you raise your overall level of playing, your ensemble playing will improve as well!

If your articulations are not working for you in a particular passage, take the mouthpiece off the trumpet and practice the rhythm on the mouthpiece alone. You will be able to easily hear any problems in your tonguing without the distraction of the full trumpet sound.

After mastering the material on your mouthpiece, return to the trumpet. You will notice that your accuracy has immensely improved!

Accuracy and Muscle Memory

To improve your pitch accuracy in a particular passage, practice the passage note by note, taking the mouthpiece off your lips between notes. Removing the mouthpiece between notes forces the embouchure (and ear) to anticipate the new embouchure position before you play the new note. You'll improve your muscle memory for each of the notes, resulting in greater accuracy for the entire passage.

It is common to crack the first note of a solo entrance when performing, especially if you're nervous. The more you use this "on again, off again" practice technique, the more you will develop your ear and muscle memory to achieve those crucial notes. "No Split Notes" (page 242) and "Accuracy Practice" (page 243) will help you build both conscious control and muscle memory, helping you achieve the right note the first time, every time!

See exercises pages 242 and 243

Buzzing on the Beach

There are many times when we find ourselves unable to practice because we are away from the instrument, on vacation, or in a quiet environment. Pocket your mouthpiece and carry it around with you for these occasions! Give your family and friends time to adjust to your new habit, which will help you keep your technique in shape even when you can't do your usual practicing. I suggest purchasing an extra mouthpiece for this purpose and keeping it in a mouthpiece pouch or case.

As you advance, use mouthpiece buzzing for extra practice during "down time."

Listen Like a Musician

Although musicality will not always arise from technical mastery, your technique will rise to the level of your musical vision. Don't focus on technique and forget the artistry!

As you listen to your playing, concentrate most on what you *want* to sound like, rather than getting used to what you *are* sounding like. Strive to improve your sound to the ideal you have in your ear. This doesn't mean you're not also listening; you need to both hear your playing as it is and have your ideal sound in your mind. It's like chipping away the marble block while imagining the finished sculpture inside.

Philharmonic Visions

To know where you are going in your practice, you need to listen to great artists performing (either live or on recordings). Over time you will begin to choose your own distinctive sound. The list of famous trumpet players on page 205 will point you toward recordings and videos that offer endless hours of inspiration.

If you are in band, it is easy to unintentionally base your standards on what you hear around you, especially when you are hearing it day in and day out! While there may be some excellent players in your band, your classmates are all still developing their own playing. Seek out trumpet performances on movie soundtracks, on the radio, and at concerts. If you take these performances as your musical benchmark, you will progress farther and faster.

Music Plus One, or Finding a Practice Buddy

Music is inherently something you do with other people, whether that's in a band hall, on a stage, or in your living room. Part of the payoff of all those hours alone in a practice room is that you get to go make great music with people!

My music experience would not have been the same without Geoff and Seth. We would go over to each other's houses, rent a movie, get a pizza for dinner, and sleep over. We practiced our band music, played our regional band music for each other, and played basketball the next morning.

We were constantly trying to outdo each other, but it was always friendly. When we got tired of practicing we would go outside and play frisbee. We showed off for each other, kept up with one another's progress, and gave each other feedback. We would even call one another up and play our newest solo over the phone.

The musical partnership with Geoff and Seth just happened; we never even thought about it. But you can create your own opportunities; you don't have to wait for fate to assign you a practice buddy! When you choose a practice buddy, look for someone you enjoy spending time with, and who has a similar level of skill and commitment. You want someone who knows when to be serious and get things done . . . and also when it's time to relax and have fun!

Meet with your practice buddy once every week or so. Prioritize the time you schedule and don't let anything else interfere with it. Like any friendship, it can be as valuable as you make it, so give it good-quality time and bring your best self to your sessions together.

When you meet with your practice buddy, work on band music, solo and ensemble music, and even private-lesson material. You can learn each other's private-lesson assignments, too. Having a practice partner is like having a study partner—it helps keep both of you motivated to do something that you sometimes don't feel like doing.

Be genuinely supportive of your friends and their playing, and be willing to be an honest critic. It's easy to get used to what we hear, and having a fresh perspective is great. You will start to notice your own mistakes and habits more once you've observed them in someone else's playing. Remember that when your friends give you feedback, it's because they want to help you grow as a player.

Since trumpet practice involves frequent breaks to allow your lips to recover, your buddy practice sessions allow you to use resting time in a musically enjoyable way. When you are taking turns with your partner, you can have a practice session that lasts two hours or more—learning the whole time but without fatiguing your lips.

Without Geoff and Seth, practicing could have gotten lonely, especially if I was tired or disappointed in my playing that day. Instead, whenever I practiced I was also wondering what they were up to. I practiced to prepare for class, but more than that, I practiced because I knew I would be seeing Geoff and Seth again tomorrow!

95

As you develop your playing and musicianship, listen to great virtuosi of other instruments as well, including violinists, singers, and other wind players. You will become aware of different aspects of the music you are playing, and their sounds will become a part of your palette of musical colors.

Don't Be Reasonable

Remember that the less you practice, the longer it will take to get better. What pieces do you wish you could already play? What would it take to get there?

If you have friends who also play an instrument, they may practice whatever amount they think is reasonable. And they will get reasonable results. If you want inspiring results, you must take your practice to a completely different level.

"There are a million things in music I know nothing about. I just want to narrow down that figure."

— André Previn

Band Class Boredom

Eric finished playing the opening to Mussorgsky's *Pictures at an Exhibition*. The five professors sitting in front of him nodded their heads. He knew what that meant. He had played a great audition at the best music school in the country, and there was a good chance he had just gotten in!

Everyone had always told Eric he could do anything he wanted to, but he didn't believe them. That is something people say to make you feel good. It might be true about other people. Definitely not him.

Eric had started playing trumpet in seventh grade. He liked the sound of the trumpet, but he hated school, and sitting still for long periods of time drove him crazy. Staying focused in band was nearly impossible, and spending an hour practicing trumpet sounded as exciting as drinking a bottle of fish oil. He lagged behind other players in his band, and considered quitting the trumpet after his first year. He stayed only because he liked being with his friends.

In his second year of band, three days before the fall concert, Eric was working on a hard passage at home and remembered his teacher's voice saying, "Listen to what you're doing!" He played the passage again and listened, expecting to hear the familiar cracked notes and mistakes. Instead, he was surprised to realize, "I sound pretty good!"

Eric began taking his playing more seriously, and found ways to channel his nervous energy when he was practicing and performing. As he learned to focus and concentrate in band, his grades went up in other classes and he actually started enjoying school.

Eric began as a below-average player with a pretty bleak future as a trumpeter. He is now studying at one of the best music schools in the country.

When he looks back at that first year of band, it is as though he is now witnessing a completely different person—but walking around in his sneakers! In a single moment, Eric woke up to his own potential. Nothing would ever be the same again.

Set your own standard. Commit to a higher goal than you think you can achieve, and then do whatever it takes to get there. It may take time to get to the ultimate goal, but other noteworthy results will begin showing up much sooner and let you know you're on course.

Strength and Range

In a perfect world, you could blow into your trumpet and a clear, beautiful, bell-like note would come out every single time. Effortlessly.

In the real world, mastery over a brass instrument means training your ear and technique to achieve perfect accuracy across the range of the trumpet. As you continue advancing in your playing, you will break through your own barriers, both physically and mentally. You have passed the point where everything is brand new, from pressing valves to reading notes. You are now beginning to train like an athlete, reaching extraordinary levels of performance with discipline, practice, and passion.

Anatomy of the Embouchure

When you buzz, three sets of muscles are working in harmony together: the *buccinator, orbicularis oris,* and *depressor labii inferioris* (Figure 9.1). These muscles play a complementary tug-of-war with one another, shaping the embouchure in precise ways across various registers and volumes as you play. With the muscles flexed and contracted, your airstream then blows the lips apart and excites them into a buzz.

The orbicularis oris is the circular muscle that surrounds the mouth; you can see it at work when you purse your lips to whistle. The depressor labii inferioris is in the chin; it pulls the lower lip slightly downward when you begin to buzz. These two muscles together form the *center embouchure.*

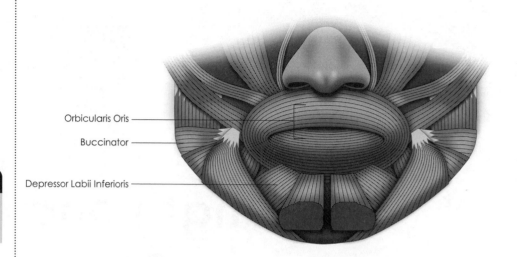

Orbicularis Oris ——————

Buccinator ——————

Depressor Labii Inferioris ——————

FIGURE 9.1

The primary embouchure muscles used to play the trumpet.

98

See exercise page 217

The buccinator is your cheek muscle. It flexes outward from the center of the lips, pulling back the corners and slightly flattening and thinning the lips. As you play, the buccinator keeps your corners firm and anchored.

It is primarily your center embouchure muscles that create the perfect tension for the various notes you play; the corners provide support and allow your lips to maintain the correct shape. No matter how much you tighten your corners, having a limp center embouchure will cause your sound to be airy, fuzzy, and unfocused, and will prevent you from reaching the higher notes on the trumpet.

Your embouchure muscles are at the heart of your physical workout on the trumpet! See page 217, "Endurance," for specific ideas to strengthen your embouchure.

Dizzying Heights, Healthy Lips

Just as athletes develop their physique over years of intensive training, so must trumpet players develop the muscles used to play in the high and low range over several years of study. When an amazing trumpeter pops out a few screaming high notes without breaking a sweat, we may pretend that it's magic or some special talent; however, those few notes are the product of many hours holed up in a practice room.

So . . . how do you improve your high range? The answer is constantly and gradually.

In the world of athletics, weight training breaks down the muscles, which then heal and strengthen on your "off" days. Your embouchure muscles need sufficient rest as well; overworking them will produce more fatigue than results. Any demanding high-range workout should happen every other day. Rest often

"The journey is the reward."

—Chinese Proverb

How High Is High?

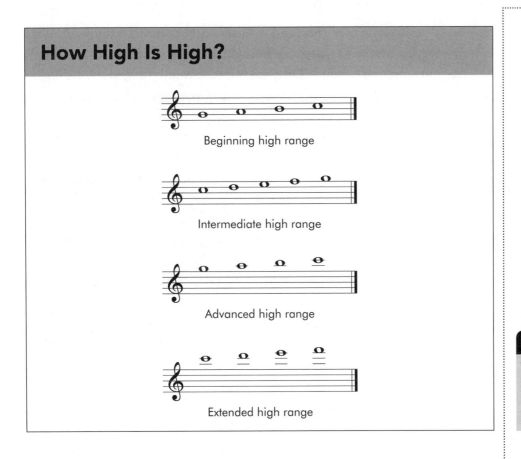

Beginning high range

Intermediate high range

Advanced high range

Extended high range

FIGURE 9.2

With practice and training, notes that used to be high for you will move into your comfortable playing range.

99

to give your lips time to recover and help you steer clear of soreness, bruising, and fatigue.

As you work on increasing your range, challenge yourself, but don't strain to play notes that are far beyond your comfort level (see Figure 9.2). When you struggle and strain, you're spicing up your high range playing with a whole lot of stress—and very likely some bad habits as well! As you develop your wind capacity and embouchure strength over time, the highest note in your range will gradually get higher, and notes that used to be hard will be easy and comfortable for you.

Vaulting into the Stratosphere

The more accurately you are able to hear each note in your mind before you play, the more accurately your embouchure will be able to quickly move into the correct formation. Sound like magic? Perhaps, but this is magic that you can count on. When you can mentally re-create the sound and feel of each high note, you will hit them accurately.

Your tongue will rise slightly in your mouth as you move to higher notes. This should happen naturally, but you can try doing it consciously if you keep

"If you don't come with discipline in your soul, somebody's going to put it there."

— Adolph "Bud" Herseth

missing a particular note. The vowel to use when playing in the high range is "ee"—which when you're tonguing becomes "tee."

As you tense your embouchure and increase your air speed for the higher notes on the trumpet, beware of excess tension in your lips and throat, and extra mouthpiece pressure. If your lips stop vibrating or your sound is strained, try slightly relaxing your embouchure and decreasing the mouthpiece pressure. While mouthpiece pressure may initially help you get the correct note, this short-term gain comes at a steep cost to your embouchure. Instead, tighten your center embouchure, raise your tongue, and use very fast air. A slight initial puff of air can help you slur from a lower to a higher note.

"Lip Bends" and "Developing High Range" (pages 224 and 247) are designed to help you build your high range. If you are a beginning trumpet player, play only as much of each exercise as you can, gradually adding to your range over many weeks and months.

When practicing the high range, don't be afraid to really go for it. What have you got to lose? It takes very fast air to vibrate lips that have the tension required to play these notes. Blow!

See exercises pages 224 and 247

The Oft-Forgotten Low Range

Welcome to the low range! In the midst of practicing all those flashy high notes, many players forget about this little detail. Composers like to focus on the clear brilliance of the trumpet's upper and middle register, so trumpet parts do not visit the lows very often.

As a result, when you do get that occasional low note, it is likely to be very unstable. Not your shining moment!

Fortunately, regularly practicing low notes will transform a weak, wobbly entrance into a clear, controlled sound—not only in the low range, but in other ranges as well.

When playing in the low range, keep your corners anchored and your center embouchure as relaxed as possible. You will discover that playing in the low range uses a lot of air: with your lips this relaxed, there is very little resistance when you blow! Your aperture will be quite wide and your lips will vibrate freely. If you have a thin, weak sound, chances are your center embouchure is too tense. Tongue placement can also help; remember to drop the back of your tongue using the "oh" vowel.

Notice that with your tongue lower in your mouth, you'll need faster tongue movements because the tongue is at a less desirable angle to create a rapid tongue flick. In addition, the lower-pressure air in the low range doesn't push the tongue out of the way as rapidly. The combination of these two factors allows the tongue to sit longer on the hard palate (alveolar ridge), creating too much space between notes.

Are You Getting Frustrated?

How do you balance eating breakfast, getting to school early for marching band, sitting through seven hours of classes, staying after school for club meetings or marching band then waiting for your parents to pick you up, doing four hours of homework, finishing school projects, eating dinner, catching up with your family, and practicing your trumpet? Oh, wait, and spending time with friends . . . if there is any time left!

There are many answers to this question; the right strategies for you depend on your schedule, commitments, and your own particular personality. Below are some suggestions; try them and see what works.

Saved by the Calendar

Keep a schedule, and write everything down in it, including deadlines, activities, meetings, and practices. Choose a weekly or monthly format so you can get a sense of the big picture. Electronic calendars are a great tool to help you visualize your time, while a physical calendar is more convenient for jotting down notes on the fly.

Next, look at where your "crunch" periods are. You will need to either reduce some commitments during that time, or work on your projects before the crunch hits. Especially when you have only limited time to complete many projects, schedule your time in advance.

Throughout the year, use downtime to get things done. Carry around the novel you need to read and pull it out when nothing else is going on; or use time in the car to brainstorm ideas for a paper you need to write.

Homework: The Black Hole?

Develop specific times to study and practice, and stick to them. Don't allow yourself to take too much time on one specific homework assignment at the expense of other things. Force yourself to be efficient! It's easy to get in a rut and go over something again and again when in reality it's time to leave it alone and move on.

If you're someone who dallies, set a timer. When it goes off, you're done with that assignment! After a few days of working with a timer, you will begin to notice you are working more quickly and have time to spare for activities you really want to do.

It's the philosophy "Work hard, play hard!"

Give yourself a daily and weekly "to-do" list so that you clearly define what you need to accomplish and can prioritize each item on the list.

101

Having a list also can help you stop worrying, since you're not endlessly rehearsing all the things you have to do in your mind but instead going down your list and systematically finishing them.

Making Choices

Make time for your friends, but know when your practice time or studies need to come first. Don't be afraid to set boundaries when you need to get off the phone and get things done.

It is important to be able to say "no" to some things when you need more time to do other things well. You don't have to belong to every club and after-school organization—even if you're interested in all of them.

Choose a few activities and devote yourself to them wholeheartedly so that you actually have meaningful experiences that enrich your life, instead of spreading yourself thin and sacrificing quality for quantity.

Quality Time with the Music

The best time to practice is probably right after school, either in a practice room or at home. That way, you can have dinner and spend the rest of the evening on schoolwork, knowing that your practice is out of the way. After dinner is also a good time; or you can arrive at school early to practice, or use a free period.

The one thing you don't want to do, though, is save your practice for the end of the evening, after doing all your homework. You will likely end up with low-energy practices and may easily spend your whole evening on homework. This is a sure way to consistently shortchange your trumpet playing.

If you're playing a musical instrument, practicing must become a non-negotiable item in your daily schedule. Practicing is just part of being a musician; it is rarely an emergency the way other homework may be, but it will pay off only if you do it consistently.

Inspiration Follows Perspiration

Isn't it funny how the things we're good at are the same ones we enjoy?

No matter which one comes first, the enjoyment or the sense of success, the other is sure to follow. Conversely, when we fail at something, some little voice in the back of our mind consoles us, saying, "That's okay. You don't really like that anyway."

So the paradox is . . . if you aren't having fun playing music, try practicing more. Very likely you just need to experience making some genuine progress. It's hard to jump-start your practicing routine when you already have a negative attitude; you'll need to wipe your inner slate clean and commit a few weeks to the experiment—long enough to get out of the rut you are in.

If you don't practice consistently, you will continue to feel frustrated, since the music will eventually get too hard for you to play. It's no fun to watch your friends move into the more advanced band, playing challenging and interesting music and deepening their social bonds, while you hang back with the intermediate band playing music that's starting to get boring for you.

Music is most enjoyable when you can sit down and play the way you really want to!

To compensate for the lower tongue angle, put your tongue on "fast speed"!

Mouthpiece Workout

As you'll recall from the warm-up chapter, buzzing your mouthpiece for a few minutes at the beginning of your practice is a great way to loosen your embouchure and get your lips vibrating. Mouthpiece buzzing is also great training for your lips during practice, building your embouchure strength and your accuracy.

Make sure you are getting a full, clear buzz, and don't worry about making the mouthpiece buzz as loud as your trumpet sound. If you do, you will blow open the embouchure and it won't be the same embouchure you use to actually play the trumpet. Maintain a gentle, even buzz—neither soft and weak nor so loud it is unstable.

When buzzing melodies on your mouthpiece, keep your air free and relaxed, with your center embouchure making the minimum adjustment necessary to reach each note. It's like hitting the bull's-eye every time you throw a dart at a dartboard. Aim for the center of every note, and don't overcompensate when reaching for a higher or lower pitch. Once you can center each note on the mouthpiece, you will be stunned at your sound and accuracy when you add the trumpet and play the same melody.

It takes more focus and internal sense of pitch to center your notes on the mouthpiece alone; the trumpet isn't there to guide your lips to the note! For this reason, in addition to improving your tone and control, regularly buzzing on the mouthpiece will give you great intonation.

See exercise page 230

As you are mouthpiece buzzing, be alert for any "ya-ya" or scooping sounds in your playing. These sounds may come from moving your jaw unnecessarily, or from not having enough air at the beginning of the note. Many players, afraid of making mistakes, test every note softly before committing full volume, not realizing they are creating a scooping sound on each note. This is a case where the cure is worse than the illness! To correct this habit, play the "Eight On, Two Off" exercise in the back of this book (page 230), making sure to start every note with a full sound.

A final advantage of mouthpiece buzzing is that your mouthpiece is much lighter than your trumpet. Without the weight of the trumpet influencing your posture, you can use mouthpiece practice to find the sweet spot on your embouchure—the perfect place where mouthpiece meets lips.

Lip Buzzing: Extreme Chops Workout

Lip buzzing refers to buzzing your lips without the assistance of the mouthpiece or trumpet . . . in short, playing the trumpet without the trumpet. You did just a few seconds of lip buzzing when you were learning to create your embouchure, but this challenging practice technique yields many secrets to the advancing player who takes the time to study its mysteries.

Many trumpeters never work on their lip buzzing, or free buzzing, until they are running into particular difficulties with range, accuracy, or sound production. However, the buzz is the heart of trumpet playing! If you incorporate lip buzzing into your regular routine, you can increase your strength and control while catching little problems before they become big ones.

Lip buzzing requires greater strength than buzzing, because the mouthpiece is not there to support the embouchure. At the same time, paradoxically, even getting a lip buzz requires that your center embouchure be loose and relaxed. Don't be surprised if you can barely lip buzz even a few notes at the beginning—and even those notes will have a distorted sound. Over years of practice, you will develop your embouchure to the point where you can lip buzz almost any note that you can play on the trumpet.

When you lip buzz, your corners should be anchored and your center embouchure relaxed. The air should leave the lips at a single point; if it leaks out at several points, you may not be using enough pressure to seal the lips. Be sure to always work with a mirror to ensure that your face is not doing things without your permission! You want to make sure your embouchure is excellent so that you are training your embouchure muscles in the correct direction.

Buzzing Pointers and Pitfalls

Begin your lip buzzing on a low C. Keeping a stable pitch on this note will be challenging to start with! Once you've achieved this note, begin adding notes above and below, increasing your range (see page 220, "Ever-Expanding Buzz").

See exercise page 220

Do not try to lip buzz a lot higher or lower than whatever is physically comfortable for you. It won't do you any good if you're wrecking your embouchure to achieve the desired note! Range will come in time, and incorrect lip buzzing will hinder you just as surely as correct lip buzzing will train you.

Do not try to produce the same volume from your lip buzz that you would on the instrument. If you blow your aperture open too wide, you will end up straying from the embouchure you actually play with. Use fast air, but keep it reasonable. Just keep your buzz and your airstream even and steady.

Because lip buzzing is strenuous for your embouchure muscles, make sure your chops are rested when you lip buzz, and stop as soon as your embouchure starts to feel tired. This will ensure that you don't inadvertently alter your embouchure to compensate for fatigue.

Barbells with Erasers

Practicing the trumpet is where you will really build your embouchure strength, but an ordinary wooden pencil can provide a great bonus workout. It's handy when you're away from home and don't have your mouthpiece to buzz. These pencil exercises will challenge your embouchure; you may experience some discomfort or fatigue as the weaker muscles make their presence known.

Below are three exercises, moving from easiest to most difficult. Practice the pencil-holds three times a week for no longer than three minutes daily. Once you can maintain the first exercise for 45–60 seconds during each of these three sessions, begin to incorporate the second exercise every third day. Finally, when you have built stamina on the second exercise, add the third exercise so you are doing one of the workouts each day.

1. Pencil-Hold

Form your embouchure as though you were getting ready to buzz your mouthpiece. Place the eraser end of a pencil stub (sharpened to half the original length) between your lips. The eraser should be fully inserted between your lips (almost touching your front teeth), in the place where your aperture would ordinarily be. The pencil will droop slightly. Tighten your center embouchure just enough to keep the pencil from falling out of your lips.

Next, push your bottom lip upward toward your top lip and raise the pencil until it is level with the floor. You will notice a slight frown as your corners lock, supporting the center embouchure muscles, which are working hard to keep the pencil horizontal. Hold the position until your muscles are completely

105

fatigued—ten to fifteen seconds if you're doing pencil-holds for the first time, thirty to sixty seconds once you've been doing them for a while.

2. Pencil Push-Up

Place your pencil as in the first exercise, and bring it up to a horizontal position. Relax the center embouchure muscles for five seconds (the pencil will droop), then tense them for five to ten seconds (the pencil will raise). Repeat this sequence five to eight times.

3. Pencil Crunch

This is an exercise for the experienced pencil user. First, bring your pencil up to horizontal. Gradually relax the center embouchure, allowing the pencil to droop slowly. Now gradually bring the pencil up to a horizontal position, repeating ten to twenty times.

Your embouchure strength will determine your stamina in each of these exercises. As with any physical exercise, there is the possibility of overworking these muscles, leading to your embouchure being sore and stiff—so be responsible and take care of your chops! Do pencil workouts for two or three weeks, then give them a rest for a few weeks.

As your embouchure strengthens, substitute a full-length pencil for your half-size one, and increase the length of time you are doing the exercises. If you didn't already feel like you were doing strength training for your lips, this workout routine should remove any doubt!

The Perfect Note

Some people can play the trumpet. Then, there are some people who can play the trumpet! If *that* is what you're interested in, then this chapter is for you.

You will reach a point in your playing when you know how to play. The trumpet is no longer a shiny mystery but has become like a friend. You know and understand it. Certain things may still elude you—your high range has an upper limit, and your tone may not always inspire you—but you do have a sense that you know what you're doing.

Your journey from here onward will be different in many ways. Up to now, you have focused on the mechanics of playing. From this point forward, trumpet playing becomes less about notes, more about art. It is a particular way of listening, a certain relationship to sound. You will get to know your trumpet intimately—and, if you listen, study, and give yourself to the task, you will succeed in becoming *that* kind of player!

This chapter is genuinely about finding the perfect note . . . tuned, accurate, and resonant. In the first several sections of the chapter you will learn the finer points of tuning each note on the instrument. The remainder of the chapter will explore sound, accuracy, and vibrato.

Each Note in Its Place

In chapter 4, you learned how to adjust your pitch by using your third valve slide. In this chapter, you will learn a few additional ways to adjust your pitch, which will allow you to tune every note on the trumpet.

As you begin to more accurately hear your tuning, you will want to start using your first valve slide for a few notes that play a little sharp. On professional instruments, this slide is fitted with a *saddle*, or cradle-shaped fixture, in which you can place your left thumb (some instruments may have a ring instead of a saddle). To lower the pitch, simply extend the slide in the same way as you would your third valve slide (Figures 10.1 and 10.2).

FIGURE 10.1

The first valve slide, here in the "in" position.

FIGURE 10.2

Pull out the first valve slide to lower the pitch.

Isn't it great when life offers you such handy gadgets to solve your problems?

Occasionally, though, you run out of gadgets and have to do things the old-fashioned way.

Up until now, you have tightened your embouchure in order to jump to a higher note on a given valve combination. However, you can also tense your embouchure just enough to raise the pitch, but without changing notes. This is called lipping up, and is the only way to raise the pitch of the few notes that are naturally flat on the trumpet.

In addition to lipping up, you can also lip down, by loosening the embouchure slightly. This is actually a bit easier than lipping up, and typically you can alter the pitch farther in the downward direction. Since you can also flatten the pitch using your valve slides, you now have two options for correcting notes that play sharp. If your trumpet lacks a saddle or ring on the first valve slide, you will need to lip the notes you otherwise would have corrected using the first valve slide.

Table 10.1 gives you a list of all the pitch adjustments you will need to make as you play, including both valve and embouchure adjustments.

You may occasionally use one additional option to adjust the pitch: your tongue.

Just as a butter knife sometimes makes the perfect screwdriver, the tongue movement you have been using to assist you with register changes can make pitch changes, as well. You can raise or lower your tongue to make minor intonation tweaks, especially in situations where you are holding a note for several beats and need to make a very small adjustment. Raising your tongue slightly will raise the pitch, while dropping your tongue slightly will lower it.

Very fine musicians can hear when the pitch is off by tiny fractions of a step. Until then, an electronic tuner goes a long way! As you play a line of music, go slowly enough for the tuner to register each pitch. Your goal is to keep the needle centered the whole time you are playing. Work consistently with a tuner to ensure that your perceptions are correct.

As your ear develops, you will discover that you are making these tiny tuning adjustments automatically. As your embouchure strengthens, those adjustments will become easier and more accurate, too.

Tune-Up for Your Trumpet

As you work on correcting the tiny details of your tuning, there are a few steps you should take to ensure that your instrument is being fully supportive of your efforts.

First of all, check your tuning slide each time you get your trumpet out of the case, to make sure it hasn't moved since the last time you played. Otherwise

109

TABLE 10.1 Ups and Downs of Trumpet Tuning

Fingering	Note	Tendency	Correction
0		Flat	Lip up slightly
		Sharp	Lip down slightly
1		Flat	Lip up
		Sharp	Extend first valve slide
2		Flat	Lip up
1-2		Sharp	Extend first valve slide
		Sharp	Extend first valve slide
		Sharp	Extend first valve slide
2-3	All notes fingered 2-3	Slightly Sharp	Lip down or extend the third valve slide
1-3		Sharp	Extend third valve slide*
		Sharp	Extend third valve slide.
1-2-3		Very Sharp	Extend third valve slide. This note is more sharp than D and requires a greater adjustment.
		Very Sharp	Extend the third valve slide almost completely. You may also extend the first valve slide out slightly for fine adjustments to this note.

*While low G, fingered 1-3, is sharp in general, you may notice your low register is flat in general due to poor air support and a loose embouchure. To correct this, increase your air speed and tighten your embouchure slightly

110

Melody, Harmony . . . Cacophony?

Ensemble music can create an incredible musical experience, for both the performers and the listeners. An isolated melody may be enjoyable, but with the addition of full scoring and interesting countermelodies, the result is a canvas of color, texture, and expression.

Of course, that's if everyone is playing in tune. If the ensemble is out of tune, clashing notes and harmonies can create new heights of unpleasantness instead.

When you are playing in an ensemble, actively listen to yourself in relation to the people around you. If you think you are out of tune, try lipping up or down. It is your responsibility to fit into the intonation of the overall ensemble.

As a brass player, you will need to make sure you complete your personal warm-up earlier in the day, prior to the ensemble rehearsal. If your lips are tight, you will tend to play slightly sharp. If your embouchure is tired, on the other hand, you will have the tendency to play slightly flat. Developing your embouchure strength and being warmed up at the beginning of the rehearsal will go a long way toward preventing both situations.

you may discover your embouchure is quickly fatigued, as you unconsciously lip almost every note to stay on pitch!

Sometimes it pays to be a little compulsive. Whether or not you make your bed every morning, keeping your trumpet clean is an essential part of good intonation. Deposits in your horn will cause the tuning to be more variable, again causing you to make more embouchure adjustments than necessary and wonder where your endurance went. Whatever your habits are elsewhere in your life, your leadpipe should be clean enough to eat off of!

Before you begin playing after a period of inactivity, press all your valves and blow warm air into your trumpet, bringing it from room temperature up to playing temperature. Otherwise the trumpet will take several minutes to rise to the correct pitch.

Retreat of the Tuning Slide

As you may recall, when you first started playing you needed to pull your tuning slide almost all the way out. Your embouchure was relatively stiff, causing you to play generally sharp across the range of the trumpet.

As your embouchure develops, you will notice that your overall pitch will begin to drop. Check your pitch with a tuner; every couple months you may need to push in your tuning slide so that your overall pitch is on target.

Eventually your embouchure will be as supple as it is going to get, and you will settle on the "sweet spot" for your main tuning slide—approximately ½ to ¾ inch from the "fully in" position, depending on the instrument and the player.

From that point forward, you will need to use your tuning slide only to adjust for temperature variations and to match the pitch of whatever ensemble you are playing in. Your overall intonation will be fairly consistent and well-established at this point.

Tune a Lap, Not a Marathon

As an advancing trumpet player, you have already noticed that you can hear things now that you couldn't hear even six months ago—including rhythm, pitch, articulation, and other elements of your playing. This is an ongoing process; you will hear finer and finer details as you advance.

For this reason, don't worry about correcting all your intonation issues in one day. Playing in tune and with a good sound takes consistent practice and ear training. It is a process of development, not something that can happen in a few blow-out practice sessions.

Don't get lost and spend hours on tuning. Even if boredom doesn't numb your concentration, you should balance this work with other important aspects of your playing. Work on your intonation for a little while each day, and over time it will come naturally to you.

Nectar in the Middle

Now that polite society is safe from the perils of bad trumpet tuning, what's next?

The holy grail of trumpet playing, of course; the sound of Doc Severinsen shooting across the stage with laser-like brilliance, his slow jazz solos musky and dark. The ageless elegance unfolding from Bud Herseth's brass bell, warm and nuanced, unerringly controlled in every detail; Tim Morrison's golden tones rippling across a movie soundtrack like drops of sunlight.

It's all in the sound.

Besides practicing a lot and cultivating your ear, there are a few strategies that will help you create your own magic elixir. To begin with, every note on the trumpet has what we call a sweet spot. You're in the sweet spot when the note is perfectly in tune and seems to ring with the greatest resonance and projection.

Lip bends are a great exercise to train your embouchure to find the center of each pitch. Lip bends involve stretching the pitch as far upward or downward as possible so that you get a sense of the whole range of intonation for a given note. Once you have heard all the possible placements, you will discover yourself beginning to hear the very best spot to place each note—in other words, the sweet spot. Hearing the changing pitch and resonance during your lip bends is

112

"True intonation is one thing that the average listener demands of a performer."
— Rafael Mendez

the first step to being able to find the perfect placement for every note, time and time again.

As you already know, to bend the pitch upward, you will tense your center embouchure as far as possible (without going to the next overtone). To bend downward, loosen your center embouchure. You will notice that lip bends are harder upward than downward—it's easier to relax your embouchure than to contract it, especially as the notes get higher. The exercises on page 224 will focus on downward lip bends, beginning on middle G.

See exercise page 224

When practicing lip bends, first use a tuner to find the correct intonation for the desired note. Next, loosen your center embouchure to bend the note downward, keeping your air fast. Finally, return to the original note, still with fast air. You may bend the note back up slowly, or you can snap it back to center. The first type of practice will allow you to explore the resonance and hear where it centers, while the second is your rapid target practice. For the best result, begin with some slow bends, then end your lip-bend practice by snapping the notes into place.

You may notice that your sound is more clear and full upon returning to the original note after bending downward. Over time, you will develop muscle memory for where the sweet spot is, and you will discover yourself finding that perfect note with lightning-fast accuracy!

Mysteries of the Mouthpiece

Your mouthpiece has served various roles over the time you have been playing trumpet. Initially, you used it to practice buzzing your lips, then it became part of your warm-up routine to get your lips moving for the day. Now your mouthpiece will begin to take on a different role: it is about to become your best friend in elevating the overall level of your technique.

When you run into a passage with difficult intervals or leaps, or are having trouble with your intonation, first play the passage on your trumpet. Then play the same passage slowly on your mouthpiece alone, centering each pitch as quickly as possible. This will be more difficult, since you don't have the trumpet guiding your lips and ear to each note. Keep practicing; the more you do it, the better you will get. Your tuner will allow you to tune each note exactly, rather than guessing whether you are in tune each time.

Once you have worked out the spots on your mouthpiece, add your trumpet back in. You just did the trumpet equivalent of training to run ten miles, then discovering that running just one mile is the easiest thing you've ever done!

As you are buzzing your mouthpiece, listen to the sound that is being produced. It should be full, even, and open, with no forcing and a minimum of distortion in the sound. You shouldn't hear air leaks or notice parts of your embouchure buzzing slower or faster, which creates various pitches and vibrations within the buzz. The sonority should be soft, easy, and fluffy, with no

113

harshness. Keep your embouchure as relaxed as possible, and use your air more efficiently to improve the tone of your buzz . . . and, ultimately the sound you produce on the trumpet.

As you begin to master mouthpiece buzzing, include mouthpiece practice as a part of each of the pieces you play. For example, try to play through an entire etude on your mouthpiece with the sweetness and intonation that you would expect when playing it on your trumpet.

Developing Vibrato

Vibrato is a pulsating effect produced by a musical instrument or voice. It is actually a regular alternation between a higher and lower pitch, producing a subtle undulation in the sound. You may begin learning vibrato once your technique is firmly established, probably sometime during your second year of playing.

Hand vibrato is a motion that pulls the mouthpiece away from the embouchure. Although it is still used by many players, we will not discuss the technique here. Embouchure or jaw vibrato is created by slightly lowering and raising the jaw. Since it uses smaller muscles, you can exert finer control over the vibrato using this method, lending greater finesse to your playing.

Vibrato on a brass instrument will always be performed by bending the pitch slightly downward, since this is easier than bending it upward. To create a vibrato, use the syllable "yaw" (rhymes with "law") to create the pattern, "yaw-yaw-yaw-yaw."

The speed of vibrato has varied over generations and nationalities of trumpeters. Currently, a vibrato that is considered expressive but still tasteful pulses approximately five times per second—possibly a little faster or slower depending on the speed of the passage and the desired intensity. A vibrato that is too rapid will sound nervous, while a vibrato that is too slow will sound uncentered and wobbly.

Spend 5–10 minutes a day practicing the vibrato exercises below:

1. After your warm-up, return to long tones, this time with vibrato. Use a metronome at sixty beats per minute; your goal should be four to six cycles per beat.
2. Once you have a working vibrato, add it to half notes (and longer notes) in your songs.
3. Once you are comfortable with half notes, add vibrato to your quarter notes.
4. When you're ready, practice slow, lyrical pieces, such as Concone's *Lyrical Studies* or Bordogni's *Melodious Studies*.

Listen to your teacher and other performers to hear ways of using vibrato tastefully and expressively. Mold your own vibrato to the sound that you most enjoy. Once you have achieved control over the speed, you can begin to add your own nuances and expression in individual phrases. For example, when you hold a long note, you may vibrate slowly at the beginning, increase the speed in the middle, then relax the vibrato at the end, as though the emotion heightens and then subsides.

In this stage of your playing, your sound is becoming more individualized, and ultimately you will develop your own musical fingerprint.

Mastering the Mind

Have you ever had one of those days when you think your tuner is purposely thwarting you? You play your solo ten times, and every single time it's as though you're throwing darts blindfolded. You hope that someday, by magic or miracle, the phrase will get in tune and stay in tune.

Hitting one note high, the next note too low, some players spend hours with a tuner, fruitlessly guessing where the next note is going to fall. If this sounds like you, here are a few techniques that can make a big difference.

First of all, your pitch will be only as good as your imagination. If you're not actively visualizing—or auralizing—the next note you're going to play, it's not likely to come out of your trumpet. Many times, we operate reactively; a note comes out and we are pleased or displeased (or even ignore it completely).

Instead, be proactive—imagine the note before it comes out, then make it happen.

If you're casual or inattentive, you won't be able to nail the note—even if you are accurately hearing it in your mind. When you're single-minded and intentional, you have the greatest potential to be accurate.

As you advance on the trumpet, you will discover that your performance success depends entirely on your training, both physically and mentally. Your discipline, listening, and awareness will all come together to develop you into a master trumpeter.

Playing at the Extremes

Richard Wagner, a famous composer, once said, "Music is the inarticulate speech of the heart, which cannot be reduced to words, because it is infinite."

Music captures the human soul at every moment—from dull heartbreak to soaring ecstasy, driving rage to triumphant glory.

And then, of course, there are the musical fencing matches.

Like knights in shining armor headed off to tournament, players brandish their trumpets and set out on a quest for victory. Artistic sensibilities may be temporarily set aside as they dive headlong into the fray, and the motto becomes, "Higher, faster, louder!" This is the animal kingdom, after all.

Whether you are delicately sculpting your *Scheherazade* solo or trying to overawe your stand partner with your towering virtuosity, you will need to develop fine control to accurately reach every note in the trumpet at every volume. This chapter is about the extremes of volume and range—improving both your soft and your loud playing, and increasing your sound and accuracy in both the high and low range.

Hazards of Playing Soft

When the music was handed out for the regional band audition last year, my students all rushed to practice the first required excerpt—the one with about 5,000 sixteenth notes.

Little did they know, their other required excerpt—the lyrical one—offered perils of a completely different nature. Marked "pianissimo," its sweet winsomeness was a worthy opponent most of them had never encountered before.

For example, there is nothing quite like playing a quiet passage and discovering that your embouchure has suddenly quit vibrating!

The aperture in soft playing is so small your lips will almost completely touch. Because of this, you need to have fast air, which will keep your aperture barely open enough to achieve your desired dynamic, while also keeping your lips in motion. Unless you develop this ability in your practice, you may have a surprise awaiting when you perform!

As you play softly, keep your mouthpiece pressure to an absolute minimum. With so little air to begin with, too much mouthpiece pressure can also cause your lips to stop vibrating. Keep the airstream constantly moving outward to avoid any shakiness or wobbling. Your sound should always have a warm core; don't get so quiet that your sound becomes wispy and brittle.

Having dry or chapped lips may also be an issue in soft playing. When your lips are dry, they are stiff and do not vibrate as freely as usual. As a temporary solution, lick your lips before you play; once you are done with your playing session, apply lip balm and make sure you're drinking enough water.

As part of your regular practice, play your etudes and exercises both at full volume and also very quietly, on either the trumpet or the mouthpiece alone. "Extreme Dynamics," page 222, will get you started.

Then, when your music gives you that occasional hushed solo, there won't be those awkward little silences.

See exercise page 222

Power and Clarity

It is exciting to play loud—it's what we're known for, right? However, please exercise some restraint, hard as it may sometimes be.

When playing forte, it's easy to think that more effort equals more sound. However, whenever you push or force, the extra tension in your body will end up squeezing the sound instead. It might be loud, but it won't be beautiful. Use full breaths and stay relaxed.

Similarly, don't let yourself get too caught up in the sheer volume; you will end up with a wild, untamed sound rather than memorable music. Any time your tone starts to break apart, you need to back off a bit till the sound is clean and clear again.

When playing at louder dynamics, your aperture will be very open and a large volume of air will be passing through your lips into the instrument. Your airstream will also be faster than for softer playing. Relax your center embouchure as much as possible: the more freely it vibrates, the greater your endurance and resonance will be. Keep your mouthpiece pressure to a minimum to allow your lips to resonate freely; this will increase your endurance as well.

Four and a Half Minutes, One Breath

The next time you are online, pick up a recording of Wynton Marsalis playing a piece by Nicolò Paganini. The piece is called *Moto Perpetuo*—which means "perpetual motion."

Wynton plays the entire piece in one breath.

Well, not exactly.

Circular breathing is a technique used to produce a continuous sound, without the interruption of taking a breath through the corners. The trumpeter stores an amount of air in his cheeks, then uses the cheek muscles to push the air from the mouth into the trumpet . . . while breathing in through the nose at the same time!

I know, I know. It sounds impossible, right?

You will never find a band or orchestra piece that calls for circular breathing; but it is a great trick to impress your friends.

To teach yourself circular breathing, get yourself a glass of water three or four inches deep. Place a standard drinking straw in the water and blow bubbles. Now, use your cheek muscles to push air out, while breathing in through your nose at the same time. The goal is to keep the water continually bubbling.

If you inhale a bit of water the first couple times, don't worry. Everyone does. You won't drown, and you will get the hang of it.

Once you have mastered the water technique, apply your new skill at the trumpet. It will be different because of the pressure needed to move air through the instrument, but if you keep at it, you will eventually learn to do it.

At that point, you can add circular breathing to your repertoire of silly human tricks.

The people sitting in front of you in band are experts in loud trumpet playing. It is their hair that will be curling if your sound is less than beautiful!

Gently with the Bell

Now that you are gaining control over the louds and softs of your playing, you are in a position to hear how your own dynamic fits into the overall musical context. This includes being aware not only of your own sound production, but also of the physical space and the players around you.

The sound of some musical instruments radiates more or less equally from all sides of the instrument. The trumpet sound, in contrast, emanates from the front of the bell, expanding outward in a cone shape. If your bell is pointed toward the floor, walls, or music stand, your listeners will perceive your sound as more covered. You wouldn't ordinarily play like this, but it can create the perfect effect in a lyrical passage, when you want a warmer sound.

As you play, begin to notice the balance between you and other players, and also the characteristics of the physical space you are playing in. In band or orchestra you can point your bell directly ahead, since the audience is relatively far enough away and the softer instruments (including the strings and many woodwinds) are closer to the audience than you are, so you will not overbalance them. Aim your bell a little higher than usual if you want to project more in a very loud passage, and raise your tongue (in the "tee" direction) for a brighter sound. In jazz band you will usually want your trumpet pointing straight out, since the trumpet is almost always the lead voice.

For softer or more lyrical passages, you might direct the bell slightly downward and lower your tongue in the "toh" direction to create a warmer, softer sound. An oblique (indirect) bell placement will take the edge off your articulation and your sound, matching the overall mood.

In a chamber setting with a smaller performance space and only a few performers, you want to adjust your volume both for the balance of the chamber group and also out of consideration for the audience. You want them to leave talking about how good you were, not how loud you were! In this setting, sit with your side to the audience, point your bell toward the floor, or both.

Don't Blame Your Mouthpiece!

Students occasionally want to experiment with a shallower mouthpiece to achieve their desired high range. While the desire for a shortcut is understandable, this is not the best way to go about developing your high range. Instead, work to expand your range to a high F on your standard mouthpiece.

While a specialized mouthpiece may give you some short-term results in the high range, it may also interfere with your sound development, and you may experience accuracy problems when you return to your standard mouthpiece.

Shallow-cup mouthpieces are best saved for use in extremely high playing (double G and above) by advanced players whose embouchure is very well-established. If you do choose to use a specialty mouthpiece for specific playing situations, ask a professional for tips and techniques about switching back and forth.

Trying Too Hard

You know how you get a new piece of music, and look for all the high notes? You go home and practice, then walk into band and sit down in your chair. You warm up, perhaps play the passage a few times as everyone else is unpacking. The director announces the piece; the baton goes down. You know exactly where the high notes are, and you are waiting for them.

The big moment comes and . . . nothing.

You just missed the note you have been preparing to play for the last thirty minutes. What happened?

First of all, being so focused on the high note and nothing else is a great way to put a whole lot of unproductive pressure on yourself. Second, in technical terms, you probably pushed so hard for the high note that you blew your aperture open too far, altering your embouchure and making it impossible for the high note to speak. Back off slightly and narrow your airstream; the high note will pop right out. Of course, don't back off so much that the high note is softer—just enough for it to speak easily.

The opposite holds true for playing in the low range of the trumpet. For low notes, if you slightly increase the volume of air you are using, the greater air volume will widen the aperture, giving you your low note. This goes a bit against what you might intuitively do. Again, use good taste; make sure you don't blow so hard that the low note is louder than the rest of the passage.

In other words, if you're going for a high note, back off just a bit; if you're going for a low note, go for it!

Lowest of the Low

Have you ever stood outside the door of your trumpet teacher's studio and been mystified by the strange foghorn sounds emanating from within? It is the kind of sound that makes you wonder whether, when you pass through the door, you will be transported into a chapter of *Moby Dick*.

As you already know, the lowest note you can play on the trumpet and cornet is low F♯. Now we're going to talk about all the notes lower than that.

You could say these notes don't quite exist; you will never see them written in a trumpet part. Pedal tones are the result of a particular acoustical property of wind instruments; including them in your trumpet practice is incredibly useful for developing a warm, centered sound. Learning to relax your embouchure for pedal tones will allow it to resonate more in general and will give you a warmer sound in the low register specifically. Pedal practice will help you eliminate tension in your playing, increasing your endurance in all ranges of the trumpet. It will also help you achieve excellent use of your air, since pedal tones require so much of it.

"If the lips remain flexible and the tone is not forced, it will be possible to play easily any note, regardless of register."

— Herbert L. Clarke

121

Basic Physics of a Brass Instrument

Are you someone who is fascinated by how things work? Then this section is for you! If not, no worries. The information below is purely to satisfy those of you who like physics or are simply curious. Skipping this section will have absolutely no implications for your career as a trumpet player!

How is sound produced on a brass instrument? While the answer to this question is mathematically complex, here is a basic explanation.

What Is a Sound Wave?

Imagine two people holding a bungee cord on both ends. When you flick your end of the cord, a ripple travels down the cord, reaches the other person, then travels back toward you. This is called a *transverse wave*. It is called "transverse" because the ripple itself is vertical (like the waves you see in the water), but it is moving horizontally.

A sound wave is similar, except that it is a *compression wave*. Its wavelength is the distance from one burst of compressed air to the next. The air between these bursts has a lower density (see Figure 11.1). Keep in mind that the bursts we are talking about are very fast! Tuning A, or A440, has a frequency of 440 bursts per second. Its wavelength is .78 meters, or about 30 inches. High notes have short wavelengths and high frequencies, while low notes have long wavelengths and low frequencies.

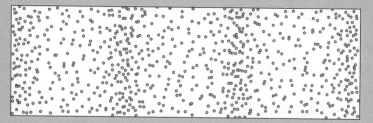

FIGURE 11.1

In a compression wave, air molecules alternate between high and low density.

Waves in a Brass Instrument

In a brass instrument, the vibration from your lips passes down the length of the tubing and bounces back when it reaches the outside air (at the bell). The interaction of vibrations up and down the tube has a strange result: the density of air stays the same at certain locations inside the instrument! These points are called *nodes*. A sound wave whose nodes stay in the same place is called a *standing wave*.

Due to some fascinating mathematics that are best saved for your advanced college physics class, all tubes also produce a wave whose length is twice as long as the tube itself. The frequency of this sound wave is called the *fundamental frequency*. The nodes in the tube are multiples (called *overtones* or *partials*) of this frequency.

More Valves, More Waves

When you press a valve key on the trumpet, the valve opens a length of tubing. This tubing increases the overall length of the trumpet, lowering the fundamental frequency. The C trumpet fingered open (no valves) has the fundamental frequency of the C an octave below the staff. When you open the second valve, the new fundamental is one half step lower. The first valve lowers the fundamental a whole step.

Just as each valve combination yields a different fundamental frequency, so each valve combination has its own overtone series, whose pitches ascend in a predictable pattern. The diagram below shows the first seven notes of the overtone series based on each fingering (Figure 11.2). The fundamental of each of these overtone series is an octave lower than the lowest note printed.

Since the intonation varies on some of these overtones, do not use this illustration as a fingering chart—use the one at the back of the book (page 212) instead!

As we mentioned earlier, the fundamental frequency is a *very* long sound wave—twice the length of the tubing! In fact, this sound wave is so long that it extends past the flared bell, rather than bouncing back—which means it's not a standing wave. Because of this, these very low notes sound different from all the others in the overtone series—they lack the clarity and resonance of higher notes.

The fundamental frequencies on a trumpet have a special name. They are called pedal tones!

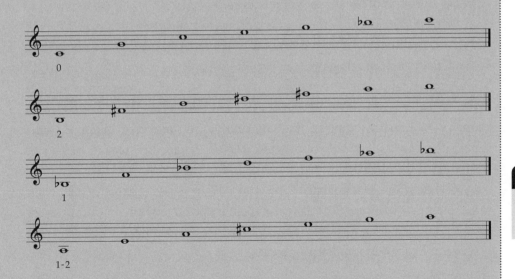

FIGURE 11.2

The harmonic series is responsible for the notes produced on each valve.

Surprisingly, pedal tones work to increase your high range as well. The precise embouchure control needed to play and tune a pedal note is the same as that needed to play high notes. The more you practice pedal tones, the more you will notice an increase in the ease and playability of your high range.

Because pedal tones are below the normal playing range of the trumpet, it may sound like a crazy idea to make a beautiful sound on these notes . . . especially after you try a few! You will initially find that your intonation has just gone out the window and the notes sound airy and fuzzy. However, you have been training your embouchure and your ear for a year or two already, and you have all the skills you need to develop this struggling sound into a warm, steady tone.

The easiest way to play your first pedal tone is to play low F♯ (fingered 1-2-3) with the third valve slide in its resting position. Next, play F♯ with the third valve slide fully extended, then lip down the F♯ to play pedal F. You have just played your first pedal tone!

From here onward, you will finger pedal tones the same way you would finger the note an octave higher. Once you have found the pedal F a few times using the altered fingering, play the same note using the traditional fingering (first valve).

Pedal tones require a tremendous relaxation of your embouchure, a very large aperture, and the lowest possible tongue position. In order to get your embouchure to vibrate in this relaxed state, you will need fast air, and a lot of it. As always, your tone quality will let you know when your technique is on the right track.

Make sure you do not break, reset, or reconfigure your embouchure to play these notes. You might consider using a mirror for this; even when your embouchure is correct, it will feel completely strange, because your aperture is so wide! Exercise control over these notes as much as possible, even with the extreme looseness of the center embouchure.

Some players may use shortcut fingerings to help lower the pitch. This will not harm anything, but it does defeat the purpose. The real goal is embouchure control, not just producing a particular note.

A tuner can come in handy when practicing pedal tones, since you are probably not used to centering pitches this low. Don't rely solely on the tuner, though—continue listening so that you internalize the correct pitch. Play the note in the lowest octave of your regular playing range, then play its pedal and try to match the pitch.

See exercises pages 245 and 249

Use the exercises on pages 245 and 249 to practice your pedal tones. James Stamp's *Warm-ups & Studies* also includes pedal tones in practically every exercise, and is a great resource for pedal practice. Over time, the pedal register will become easy and familiar to you.

Trumpets and Mouthpieces

It was the fall of eighth grade, and my parents had ordered me a new case for my trumpet because the old one was cracked. As I was sitting upstairs doing my homework, my parents yelled for me to come down to the kitchen. Sitting on the table was a brand-new Bach trumpet case, wooden, with leather trim and brass fittings.

My parents told me to open the case—they had put my beginner trumpet in it and wanted to make sure it fit. I opened the case.

Inside, where my old beginner trumpet should have been, was my Dad's silver Bach Stradivarius.

Except it wasn't my dad's, they told me. They swore it was a new trumpet for me.

I didn't dare believe them; it sounded too good to be true. They protested and persuaded, and I refused to believe them. I couldn't bear to be disappointed about something like that.

It took them ten minutes to convince me, but finally I accepted the crazy, exhilarating truth . . . my parents had gotten me a professional trumpet! For months I cleaned that trumpet every time I got a fingerprint on it. It was a sign that my mom and dad believed in my playing and trusted me to do something with it.

Earn Your Horn

If you are just starting on the trumpet, a beginning-model instrument will more than meet your needs; it is more affordable, and the capabilities of a professional trumpet won't be accessible to you yet. After about three years of playing, you will probably be ready for a professional-level instrument. If you are taking lessons and have been serious about practicing, you may be ready for a professional trumpet sooner.

Not Just for Professionals

Many brass instrument makers sell three lines of trumpets: beginner, intermediate, and professional. With many makes and models available, from brass to silver to gold plated, which one is best for you?

Often the only difference between a beginner and intermediate trumpet is the price. Both beginning and intermediate instruments have a two-piece bell and are made in large quantities.

Although professional trumpets are partially machine-made, the valves and slides on these instruments are hand-fitted. You will notice that the third valve slide on professional trumpets moves effortlessly and that the valves are more fluid, and their one-piece bells provide better projection and responsiveness than two-piece bells. The valves on a professional trumpet are made of *monel*, a metal alloy composed of nickel, copper, and trace amounts of iron and manganese. Monel is resistant to corrosion and is ideal for a high-moisture environment.

Once you've outgrown your first instrument, the wisest choice is to simply buy a professional trumpet and be done with the step-up process. You will get a trumpet that is genuinely superior to your first instrument, and the resale value of a professional trumpet will be much higher than that of an intermediate trumpet.

It's Still Brass under There

Are you playing a beat-up, old beginner trumpet and counting the days until you can trade it in for your new instrument?

If you are, slow down a bit. All trumpets are made out of brass, no matter what their surface plating. Most current research shows that silver plating on a trumpet does not affect the instrument's performance.

The most important element of your playing is how you sound, not how you look. Before you set your heart on any particular instrument, remember that you can silver-plate just about anything. Just because a trumpet is silver-plated does not necessarily mean it is a high-quality instrument. Many students have inherited a trumpet that was in their family. Their old, tarnished

Everything You Need to Know about Trumpet Mutes

A *mute* is an object inserted in the bell of a trumpet that muffles the instrument's vibrations. Although mutes will make the trumpet quieter, their primary purpose is to alter the tone color in some desirable way. Most mutes will affect the intonation somewhat, so work with a tuner to stay on pitch.

Mutes may be made from cardboard, aluminum (brighter sound), brass or copper (darker sound), synthetics or polymers, or any combination of these. Mutes may even be made from cloth bags, or any other soft material that yields the desired sound quality.

Many a quiet moment during a concert has been jarred by the inadvertent fall of a mute! Use a mute rack or, during quick mute changes, use the pit of the arm. If you don't have a mute rack, place a towel on the floor, then place mutes on the towel.

To place your mute, blow warm air into the inside of the bell to create condensation. This will help the cork stay in place. Mute placement and rotation may affect the sound, so experiment for the best position.

Among all the various types of mutes listed below, the general qualities that make a good mute are (1) consistency in all pitch and dynamic ranges, (2) ease of airflow, (3) stability in the trumpet bell, (4) minimal change in intonation, and (5) desired sound quality and volume.

Since trumpet cases don't usually have space for mutes, you might consider a mute tote bag (pictured above) to help keep them in good condition. These bags are relatively inexpensive and can be used for other accessories as well.

Straight Mute

This mute may be either cone- or pear-shaped and is the first mute a student should buy. You will probably want an aluminum straight mute to start with. A straight mute may make your trumpet play sharp, so move your tuning slide out a bit.

127

Cup Mute

Another must-have for any trumpeter, cup mutes come in various materials and forms; the sound color is changed by moving the cup. If the cup is adjustable, the player can move the cup while keeping the cone fixed in the bell, keeping the intonation stable. The mute may tend to play slightly sharp, but will go flat if the cup is moved very close to the bell.

Practice Mute

Useful for when you don't want to disturb family or roommates late at night, practice mutes cut the sound by 70 percent or more! Since this is a type of straight mute, it may cause you to play sharp; use your tuning slide to compensate.

128

Plunger Mute

Used mainly by jazz musicians, a plunger mute is most often a (clean) rubber household plunger. They are also available in aluminum with a flock-sprayed interior. Of the several available sizes of rubber plungers, choose the size closest to the diameter of the trumpet bell. These mutes may cause the trumpet to play flat.

Harmon, or "Wa-Wa," Mute

Used primarily by jazz musicians, "wa-wa" mutes greatly reduce the volume and produce a distant, buzzy sound, requiring a lot more air to play. The mute has two separate parts: the body (a funnel-shaped portion that inserts into the bell) and the stem (a removable tube). You can play with only the mute body in the trumpet, or you can create the wa-wa effect by opening and closing your hand over the stem while it is placed in the mute body. The mute may tend to play sharp.

Cloth Bag Mute

Used mainly by jazz musicians, cloth bag mutes give the trumpet a soft, velvety tone. The cloth may be draped partway over the bell, or the bell may be placed fully inside the bag. The cloth bag may cause the trumpet to play flat.

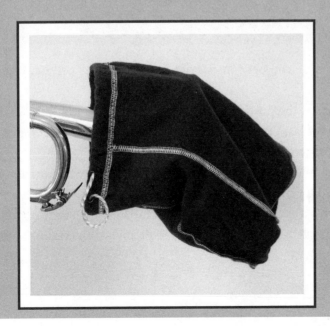

instrument may play circles around a shiny new beginner instrument! A higher-quality finish on the trumpet will improve the visual appearance of your instrument, and that's it.

While you can't tell a trumpet's quality from its finish, good trumpet manufacturers do tend to reserve their silver plating for their professional trumpets. First, this sets their professional trumpets above their student models. Second, silver-plating a beginner trumpet would be a waste of money and silver. Some manufacturers silver-plate their beginning models and call them intermediate models. If you are ready for a better trumpet, buy a professional instrument from a high-quality maker and avoid wasting money on one of these instruments.

My advice to you is to buy a high-quality trumpet with a beautiful sound, regardless of the finish, and regardless of minor cosmetic wear. The finish serves to protect you from touching raw brass as you play, and to protect the brass from the acid in your hands and other elements in the environment. The rest is purely eye candy.

Almost Factory-Tuned

Although it seems like a new instrument from a good manufacturer should have excellent intonation, small errors can occur during the construction process that cause the trumpet to play out of tune. It is not uncommon, for example, to find excess solder in the joints of your trumpet. There may be other flaws as well; for example, the bore may be too large, or some parts may fit incorrectly.

As you test a new trumpet, have a tuner nearby, and pay attention to your intonation. If it does not play at least as well in tune as your previous instrument, or if particular notes are more out of tune than you would expect (review

Building the Bell

The bell of the trumpet consists of two sections, the bell stem and the bell flare.

The *stem* is the portion of tubing that leaves the first valve slide, all the way up to the last three inches of the *bell* (the business end of the trumpet). These last three inches are called the *flare*.

On beginner instruments, the bell and the flare are made separately, then joined together in a process called *brazing*. The seam is then filed and sanded until it is completely smooth to the touch. Once the surface of the trumpet is plated with another layer of metal, the seam is completely hidden!

Shopping for a Trumpet?

- Compare at least two or three different brands (e.g., Bach, Yamaha, and Schilke) so you have a sense of the different trumpets that are available.
- Once you have chosen a brand, you may want to try different bell weights. You will most likely want a medium-weight bell, which is suited for most playing situations.
- Buy your trumpet from a reputable store or from someone you trust to be honest with you. Make sure it has a warranty (for new instruments) or a fair return policy (for used instruments).
- The sound quality should be 90 percent of your concern as you try different instruments. You should like the trumpet's appearance, but sound is everything!
- Make sure the trumpet is in good working condition.
- Have your director or private teacher listen to your new trumpet. He or she will hear different things in front of the bell than you hear as you play.
- Some instruments come with what manufacturers call a "signature model" mouthpiece, designed to enhance some particular quality of that instrument. That's fine, but use your own mouthpiece until you've adjusted to the new trumpet. You can change mouthpieces later if you wish.
- Request a one-week trial period to test the trumpet. Use this time to honestly evaluate your purchase and make sure it suits your playing and personality.
- Don't hesitate to change your mind during this period. For this much money, you need to be happy!

the intonation section of chapter 10), you need to return the trumpet to the store while you are still within your trial period.

One Mouth, Many Mouthpieces

As you progress in your trumpet studies and need to achieve a fuller sound, you will want to increase the inner-rim diameter of your mouthpiece. If your embouchure is sufficiently well developed, you can move from your initial Bach 7C mouthpiece to a bigger mouthpiece such as a 5C or 3C. This new mouthpiece should carry you well into advanced playing.

Many Shades of Brass: The Trumpet Family

B♭ Trumpet

The most common trumpet used by amateurs and professionals alike is the B♭ trumpet. In the late nineteenth century, the B♭ trumpet began to replace the then-standard F trumpet in orchestras, and is most used in concert bands, jazz ensembles, and some European orchestras (along with the rotary trumpet). Many American trumpet compositions have been written for this instrument.

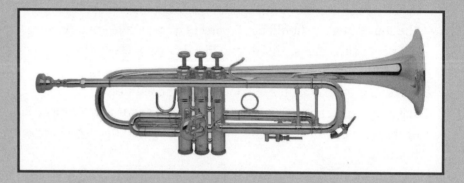

C Trumpet

The C trumpet typically produces a more brilliant tone than does the B♭ trumpet, and has a quicker response. It is widely used in the solo (especially French) trumpet literature, and since World War II has become the most commonly used trumpet in professional symphony orchestras in the United States.

Compared to the B♭ trumpet, the main concern in playing the C trumpet is intonation. The top space E, which would be fingered open, should be fingered 1-2 to prevent it from being extremely flat, except in fast passages, where speed is more critical than pitch. Similarly, the note E♭, which would be played second finger, must be played 2-3 on the C trumpet for the same reason, with the exception of fast passages.

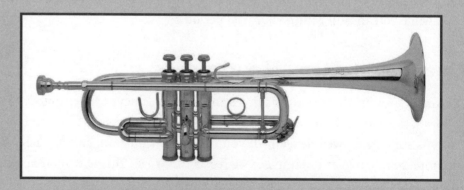

Cornet

More compact in appearance than a trumpet, a cornet has a somewhat darker, sweeter sound. Articulation is easier on the cornet, and compositions written for it often use rapid passage-work similar to that written for flute. It may be used to achieve a particular color on a musical line, and students often use it for its closer center of gravity (it feels lighter to hold) and balance.

A trumpet and cornet, both pitched in B♭, are made from an equal amount of tubing and have the same fingerings; however, a greater portion of a cornet is conical (meaning the diameter of the brass tubing gradually increases). The increase in diameter may be gradual or stepped, with each piece slightly wider than the next. A modern cornet is also wrapped in larger loops, and may have a double or triple wrap entering the valve casing.

The cornet also uses a different mouthpiece: the shank is smaller in diameter and shorter in length. A traditional cornet mouthpiece has a deeper and more conical cup, bringing out the warm cornet sound.

A trend toward a brighter, more brassy, orchestral sound has led to a preference for the trumpet in most ensembles, but the cornet is still a key member of the brass band.

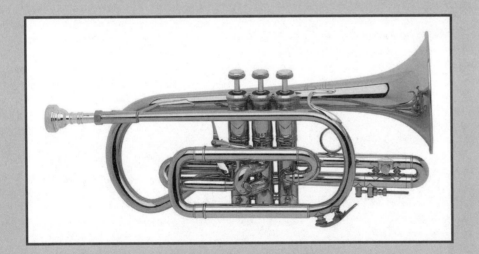

B♭ Flugelhorn

The flugelhorn has a dark, deep, full sound. Although commonly found in the jazz realm, brass bands also include the flugelhorn as a core member. It is the largest instrument in the trumpet family other than the bass trumpet (which, though rarely used, is featured in a few of Wagner's operas).

The flugelhorn may be made with a fourth, additional valve. For the correct intonation and characteristic sound, only a flugelhorn mouthpiece (which is more funnel-shaped) should be used.

133

Trumpet in E♭ (Soprano) or D

This trumpet can be pitched in two different keys, E♭ or D, with the use of various slides and a removable bells. It uses the standard trumpet mouthpiece. When used in a brass band, the E♭ trumpet is called a soprano trumpet.

The E♭ side of the trumpet is most commonly used for the performances of the Haydn and Hummel trumpet concertos, and for some twentieth-century solo works. It is used in occasional orchestral passages for its sound and vibrancy.

The D side of this instrument is used primarily for Baroque orchestral works on the third trumpet part. This instrument may also be used in orchestral playing for passages that are difficult to finger quickly on a C or B♭ trumpet.

Usually made with three valves, the D/E♭ trumpet has the same intonation issues as the C trumpet. The alternate fingerings suggested for the C trumpet (see above) can be implemented here as well. The addition of a fourth valve extends the lower range by a fourth and allows for intonation corrections in higher ranges, using alternate fingerings.

Rotary-Valve Trumpet

The rotary-valve trumpet uses rotors instead of pistons to change the length of the tubing. Compared to the piston trumpet, it has wider curves, requiring good breath support to play and giving it a somewhat darker sound. The rotary valves respond slightly more slowly than piston valves, a difference noticeable primarily in fast passages.

Orchestras that do not ordinarily use a rotary-valve trumpet may use it for works by nineteenth-century Germanic composers such as Beethoven, Brahms, Bruckner, and Strauss; and the instrument is generally preferred in German orchestras.

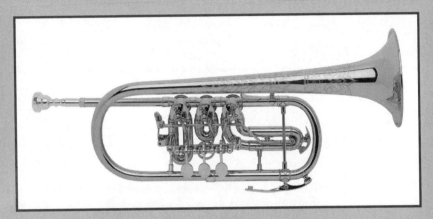

Trumpet in E, F, and G

This trumpet can be pitched in E, F, or G with the use of removable slides and bells. Historically called the *sopranino* trumpet, many players refer to it as a piccolo, even though it is pitched lower than the standard piccolo (which is in A or B♭). Some models add a fourth valve, extending the low range by a fourth and allowing for intonation corrections using alternate fingerings. It uses a standard trumpet mouthpiece.

The E trumpet is commonly used for the performance of the Hummel trumpet concerto in its original key. While Bach cantatas and other Baroque works are sometimes performed on the piccolo (see below), the F/G trumpet has a darker, more full-bodied sound and can make fingerings and intonation friendlier for the performer—while still giving the advantage of the higher register.

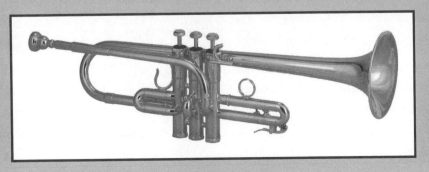

A and B♭ Piccolo Trumpet

The A and B♭ piccolo trumpets are performed most often in Baroque orchestral and solo Italian Baroque works.

The Baroque *natural trumpet* was made of a long, simply wrapped, single tube. Removable *crooks* (see page 10, "Helpful crooks") allowed the player to adjust the key. Specialized players performed in the highest register of the instrument, or *clarion*, where the notes in the overtone series are close together. At the time, that was the only way to play scale-like material on the trumpet.

The piccolo trumpet is the modern-day version of the clarion. It makes high notes much easier to play, since on the piccolo they lie in the middle of its range!

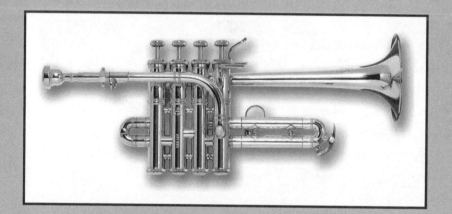

The A piccolo sounds six notes higher than printed. For example, low C (printed) will actually come out as an A. The B♭ piccolo, which sounds an octave higher than a B♭ trumpet, is most commonly used for the performance of Bach's Brandenburg Concerto No. 2 and in brass quintet music.

The mouthpiece of the piccolo trumpet may have either a cornet or trumpet shank, depending on the manufacturer. You may find the cornet shank to be more responsive.

Most modern piccolo trumpets have a fourth valve, allowing trumpeters to better execute trills and play lower on the instrument. The fourth valve also allows for intonation corrections, including for notes that ordinarily play sharp, such as 1-2-3 and 1-3. These notes can be played 2-4 and 4, respectively.

Remember that a mouthpiece can only complement your existing technique. Ideally, the perfect mouthpiece should ease your high range, blow easily and freely in the middle and low range, play in tune, help your endurance, and be physically comfortable. If you have a particular technical issue, though, your new mouthpiece isn't going to fix it.

As you move to an advanced (pre-college) or pre-professional level of playing, you may want to move to a mouthpiece with an even larger rim—for example, 1½C, 1¼C, or 1C. This larger mouthpiece will give your sound even more depth and resonance.

If you are doing lots of high-range work (for example, playing lead in a jazz band), you may want to experiment with a shallower cup (Bach sizes D, E, and F). Alternately, if you are doing serious orchestral playing, you may want to try a deeper cup (Bach sizes B and A) for a warmer, darker sound.

Although a new mouthpiece is a small investment in terms of price, the investment is high in terms of adjusting to the embouchure change over the next month. Take the time you need to make a good decision so you don't waste a month of study adjusting to a mouthpiece that ultimately does not work out.

Tips for Choosing a New Mouthpiece

- Before you try your new mouthpiece, warm up fully on your standard equipment. This will give you a reliable basis for comparison.
- Choose a room with good acoustics (it should have a good resonance when you clap your hands once and listen to the reverberation), or somewhere you are used to playing.
- If possible, have a teacher or another trumpet player with you during these trials. They will hear the sound differently standing in front of the bell than you will behind the trumpet.
- While trying your new mouthpiece, take frequent breaks so that your chops are as fresh as possible for each new mouthpiece. This allows for a fair comparison of equipment.
- Have a friend or fellow trumpet player mix up your mouthpiece choices so you are not conscious of which one you are playing. You may be surprised which one you like because it may not be the one you were hoping for.
- Once you have chosen a size that you like, try playing several of the same size. There is some variation even within each size.

137

After the Honeymoon

After a week or two of using your new mouthpiece, you will probably notice a temporary drop in your endurance and range. This is completely normal, since you are using your embouchure muscles slightly differently in the new setup. The initial excitement ("Where has this mouthpiece been my whole life?") is often followed by frustration as your muscles become fatigued. Don't worry—you will get your chops back once the muscles have rebuilt their endurance.

Before starting with your new mouthpiece, take a day or two off from playing and buzzing to give your muscles time to return to their ideal, well-rested state. If you have a band rehearsal on these days, play as little as possible. After this rest period, ease into the new mouthpiece with a warm-up of long tones.

On your old (beginning) mouthpiece, the smaller inner rim offered considerable support for your lips in forming the aperture. As you move to a larger size, the benefit is that more of your lips fit inside the mouthpiece and are now free to vibrate, creating more depth in your sound. The tradeoff, though, is that your embouchure muscles will be doing more of the work in forming the aperture, with less structural support from the mouthpiece rim. Developing these muscles will take some time, so be patient.

Practice no more than forty-five to sixty minutes daily for the first two weeks of the mouthpiece change, work with a mirror to keep your embouchure correct, and rest frequently. The reduced practice schedule will allow the muscles to gradually build endurance without being overworked. By the time two weeks have passed, your embouchure muscles should have begun to acclimate to the new mouthpiece and will have enough strength and endurance to transition back to your regular practice routine.

After all the time you've spent picking out your mouthpiece, give it a fair chance to work for you! Place your old mouthpiece somewhere you won't reach for it in a moment of frustration. If your new mouthpiece isn't working beautifully for you after a month, you can return to your old mouthpiece, or you can start your search again with a better idea of what you're looking for.

Cups, Cones, Bores, and Shanks

The flugelhorn, trumpet, and cornet are played with mouthpieces that differ in the length of the shank, the size of the bore, and the shape of the cone (see illustrations). Each mouthpiece brings out the sound that is characteristic of each instrument. Mouthpieces vary for other reasons as well. For example, mouthpieces with a shallow cup facilitate high-range playing.

Alternating from one mouthpiece to the next can take some adjusting, since each mouthpiece sits a little differently on the lips. One solution is to purchase mouthpieces for each instrument that all have the same size rim. If you are using several mouthpieces in your playing, you may consider buying a mouthpiece case that can accommodate multiple mouthpieces.

The earliest trumpet mouthpieces were simply extensions of the trumpet itself. If you think changing mouthpieces is uncomfortable, imagine playing without a comfortable, modern rim!

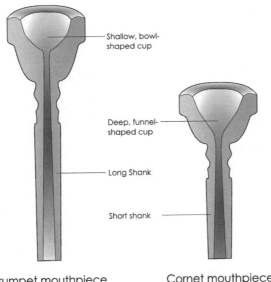

Trumpet mouthpiece   Cornet mouthpiece

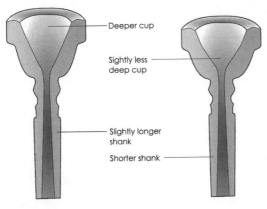

Flugel mouthpiece   Cornet mouthpiece

13

Adjusting to Braces

As a trumpet player, you probably didn't wake up one morning and think, "You know, I think braces would be a great addition to my playing!"

Much as you might not have chosen braces, chances are you are reading this chapter for a reason. So here is the scoop: Although you may wish you didn't have to deal with braces, this is just an embouchure change—not a musical disaster. Adjustment takes a little more or less time for different people, but you will adjust.

Besides the discomfort of the braces themselves, the extra metal on your teeth will change your physical relationship to the mouthpiece. Playing may be unfamiliar and difficult for several weeks—a frustrating discovery after you've worked hard to achieve your current level.

Don't be self-conscious about playing with braces. You are the only one who expects you to sound perfect all the time. Give yourself the time and space you need to figure out how to play with the new metal in your mouth.

Brackets Everywhere

While we are all familiar with the standard braces that are cemented to the front of the teeth, there are other options available. Standard braces are made of stainless steel brackets, with wires that pull the teeth into the desired alignment. Some brackets may be smoother than others, so do a bit of research before your appointment and find out what's available. Once they're cemented on your

"Music is a higher revelation than all wisdom and philosophy. Music is the electrical soil in which the spirit lives, thinks and invents."

— Ludwig van Beethoven

teeth, your braces are pretty much not going anywhere—so it pays to ask your questions well before the orthodontist is mixing the plaster.

As an alternative to metal braces, the Invisalign™ system uses clear, removable molds that are customized to correct your teeth. As the teeth move into the desired position, new molds are made, gradually achieving the desired result.

Your orthodontist doesn't put braces on trumpet players every day. They may assume that, like most patients, you want the least expensive option—when in your case, spending a little more money might make your life much easier. Consult with your orthodontist and your teacher, and keep asking questions until you are satisfied that you are choosing the best option for you.

Avoid getting braces on the upper and lower jaw at different times (a few months apart, for example). Orthodontists sometimes suggest this strategy to spread out the adjustment, but in reality you will end up making two embouchure changes instead of one. You are better off making the transition all at once.

Tough Upper Lip

Once you begin playing, those glittering little brackets are going to push themselves into your lips, and you will discover yourself fantasizing about ways to save your tender chops from this foreign threat!

While various options are available to cushion the braces, my suggestion is to put up with the discomfort rather than trying to cushion it. Anything you place on top of the braces will put even more distance between the teeth and the lips, stretching the lips and decreasing their flexibility and responsiveness.

If you play on the braces themselves, scar tissue will build up over time and create a natural cushion for you. After the initial adjustment period, you may still experience discomfort, but playing should not be painful. If the pain has not disappeared by the end of two months, consult your orthodontist; he or she may be able to adjust the braces themselves.

Besides the obvious lip irritation and soreness, you will probably notice decreased endurance, range, and flexibility for the first two months after getting braces. Don't worry—you will figure out how to play again! Practice for ten to fifteen minutes at a time, then rest and play another short session. Over time, your lips and technique will recover, and you will be relieved to sound like yourself again.

Cushioning the Blow

If you need some help coping with the discomfort of playing with braces, here are some options to make you more comfortable:

- **Wax:** Molded onto the braces to cover the sharp metal edges.
- **Denture Cushions:** Made of a cloth-like material impregnated with wax. After they have been in your mouth for a while the heat will mold them to a custom fit.

- **Braceguard™:** A putty mouth guard used to protect the lips from damage from the braces. This guard creates a custom fit and can be purchased at many music stores.
- **Morgan Bumper™:** A soft, clear material shaped into a semicylinder that slides into place over the braces.
- **Karwoski Lip Protector™:** Similar to the Morgan Bumper, this device clicks onto each individual bracket.

Some musicians just put folded pieces of plastic or paper over their teeth. Please don't do this—you could swallow or inhale these small items.

Adjusting to the Braces

Do you remember when you started the trumpet, and your lips had to figure out what in the world to do with this mouthpiece sitting on them? You may experience a moment of déjà vu when you first put your trumpet on your mouth with its new metal equipment.

Don't worry, though. Your lips spent a year or two developing muscle memory when you started playing, and you will find the new embouchure more quickly this time. You may discover, though, that you need to blow more air than before to get your lips to vibrate.

You should always brush your teeth before playing, but with braces this becomes even more important. Food particles can get trapped in the wires and quickly end up in your trumpet. You will have to clean your trumpet more often; your sound will suffer if you do not, and you do not need any more

---

Exercises for Braces

For the first week you have braces, play a chromatic scale starting on low C and going down to low F♯, holding each note for eight counts. Your lips will be less responsive with braces, so you will need to use very fast air to set them into motion. Keep the mouthpiece pressure light and play at a soft dynamic.

Next, start on low C and go up the scale chromatically, holding each note for eight counts. Don't venture too high into your range until your embouchure feels strong enough to hit the higher notes comfortably.

Play through the exercises once using a breath articulation (the syllable "poo"), then a second time using a tongue articulation ("too"). Your goals should be fast air, lip responsiveness, and repairing the tone quality if it has become fuzzy or crackly.

If you have Max Schlossberg *Daily Drills & Technical Studies*, use exercises 1–3 as an alternate to the exercises listed above.

"Music expresses that which cannot be put into words and that which cannot remain silent."

— Victor Hugo

technical challenges at this point! You may also discover you have to empty your water key more often.

Whenever you get your braces tightened, your embouchure will again change slightly. Practice long tones each time to stabilize your playing with the new adjustments.

If possible, work with your director or private instructor several times a week until you have adjusted to the braces. Your teachers will guide you into playing with braces while making sure you don't develop bad habits. The correct technique may not initially be the most comfortable one.

Stop Wiggling

You may find yourself wanting to shift the position of your trumpet according to the pain your lips are experiencing. If your top lip is getting sore, you might pivot downward. With bottom lip discomfort, the pivot would be upward.

Tips for Braces

Once They're On

Mouth workout: To get used to the sensation of braces, and to begin toughening the inside of your mouth, practice smiling widely, then quickly pursing your lips.

Smart practice: Practice for short periods of time at first. Start with ten to twelve minutes, twice a day. Then increase the time as your comfort level increases. Rest as often as you need to.

Protect your lips: Avoid excess pressure. The more pressure you put on your lips, the less responsive they will be.

Correct technique: Work with your director or private teacher. They can make sure your embouchure stays correct and help you be as comfortable as possible. Be patient! You will adjust—it just takes time.

After They're Off

Rest and relax: Allow a short amount of time to go by before practicing again. Let your body get used to having the braces off.

Smart practice: Practice for short periods of time. You want to gradually build your strength, avoiding bad habits created by trying to play on an embouchure that is weak or fatigued.

Adjusting your embouchure: Stay in communication with your director or private teacher to make sure your embouchure remains good. Proper guidance is crucial right now!

Try to leave the trumpet in the same place instead of constantly adjusting. The mouthpiece should be equally distributed between the top and bottom lips. The more tolerance you can build up in the same spot, the sooner the pain will subside.

Back to the Enamel

As you anticipate playing on unadorned teeth again, you may be imagining the blissful ease of putting on a comfortable shoe you haven't worn for years!

However, the reality is that this is a second embouchure change . . . albeit a more welcome one this time.

If possible, schedule the removal of your braces so that you have a month to adjust to the change before any performance. Summer is the perfect time for this. Work with your director or private teacher to make sure your embouchure is set up correctly as you make the transition back to playing without braces.

With your braces removed, you will now have a smooth, flat surface on which to comfortably place your mouthpiece. You'll need to get used to the mouthpiece being closer to your teeth—and, since your lips are more responsive again, you will probably discover you are over-blowing. Back off slightly, using only the air you need to achieve your sound.

Use slow practice to ease back into your playing. Remember that the braces have moved your teeth into a different place than they were two years ago! Approach your practice thoughtfully and with awareness, taking as much time as you need to adjust.

Cultivating Patience

Whether you are having braces put on or having them removed, remember that you are going through an embouchure change, and you will experience some temporary setbacks in your playing. Take your time getting used to the adjustment, and accept wherever you are in that transition.

With good practice technique and the help of your private teacher or band director, you will make the transition successfully and continue to advance your playing!

Sight-Reading

My teacher was sitting at her desk, an expression of slight dismay on her face, in spite of her best efforts.

I could hear the familiar sound of stifled laughter behind me as I struggled through a page of *The Outsiders*, reading aloud in my English class.

My mind was filled with a swirl of words; I could hear them as they left my mouth, letters and words rearranged, the scene with Darry and Ponyboy turned into verbal mincemeat. It was painful and embarrassing, and I sighed with relief when she finally moved on to another student.

On the basketball court I excelled, and I could put out a trumpet solo with brilliance and confidence. But I dreaded reading out loud.

Dr. Gresham took one look at my face when I walked into my trumpet lesson that day and asked me what was wrong. When I told him, he frowned and began pulling books from a tall stack of music and flipping the pages.

After a minute he opened an old tattered gray book and said, "Play this. Don't stop, just play."

Dr. Gresham sent me home that day with a new assignment. From then on, I would spend ten minutes of every practice playing a few lines of unfamiliar music. As I dealt with my discomfort and played the music anyway, I began to see improvement and was able to read songs that were closer to my playing level. As I progressed, I played whatever I could get my hands on; I would pull a book off the shelf in the band library and take it home with me for fresh material.

Years later, in my senior English class, the teacher asked for a volunteer to read a passage from *Pride and Prejudice*. The old middle school embarrassment was now a distant memory, and I had read the assignment and liked the book.

My hand went up, the teacher nodded at me, and I began reading aloud. The words flowed effortlessly, as though I was reciting the book from memory. I finished the passage and the teacher nodded her head approvingly.

Developing the skill of reading aloud had everything to do with me training myself to look ahead in playing music and to focus on the big picture rather than getting lost in the details. Sight-reading is not magic; like any other technique, it can be learned! This chapter will set you up to walk into any sight-reading situation with confidence and skill.

Look at the Forest, Not the Trees

Assuming you have a basic familiarity with musical notation—notes, rhythm, time signature, and key signature—you should start sight-reading about six months into your training.

When learning any language, we learn to associate certain shapes and symbols with particular sounds. Music is no different. When you first learned to read English, you pieced words together letter by letter. With music, you read note by note. With a little practice, though, you will be able to glance at a group of notes and see the overall pattern, just the way you read groups of letters as a word.

When choosing music to sight-read, you should generally choose selections that do not present new technical challenges. You should be focusing on reading the material, not developing your physical technique. Use the rest of your practice time, not your sight-reading time, to learn new technical skills or difficult music.

Don't read the same piece more than twice in one month. Remember, the material must be unfamiliar to develop your sight-reading skill! Read whatever you can get your hands on. Your sight-reading practice should be somewhere in the middle of your practice time, when you are mentally and physically warmed up but not yet fatigued.

First, Mental Practice

Before you dive into the new piece in front of you, you need to get some basic information, such as tempo, key signature, and time signature. Mentally choose a tempo and tap it to yourself while silently reading through the first couple of bars.

Now, look the composition over and identify potential trouble spots. You may need to adjust your tempo if you discover it is too fast—keep it a little on the slow side for safety. Scan the piece visually to find the fastest notes, and choose a tempo that will allow you to accurately play those notes.

Mentally visualize the sound of difficult intervals (distances between notes) and finger through any difficult spots. Count or quietly tap any

See exercise page 218

difficult rhythms. Make sure you understand where the beats are, even if the details of the rhythm are complex. "Counting Beats" (page 218) offers you a way to count that will help you to practice rhythms out loud and internalize their sound.

Don't give yourself too much advance practice, or it's not sight-reading anymore! Your preparation time should be brief—less than a minute.

Get Ahead of Yourself

As you play, look ahead as much as possible. Don't get lost in what's happening right now—looking ahead will prepare you for what's next! The faster the music, the more beats you will need to look ahead.

It is worth training yourself to look ahead no matter what. Even though concentrating on the current spot in the music might allow you to get one more correct note in this measure, looking ahead will allow you to get many more notes and rhythms correct in the next measure.

To practice looking ahead, try reading a book or magazine out loud, keeping your eyes ahead of the words that you are reading. (The exercise will work only if you read out loud; you must be saying one phrase while you're looking at the next.) This will give you an idea of how to do the same thing as you read a piece of music.

You can look ahead using your peripheral vision, or by glancing ahead then glancing back to your current spot. You will gradually be able to remember and play what you just saw, while your eyes have moved on.

No Note Is an Island

Train yourself to see rhythm in beats, rather than individual note values. Focusing on individual notes can cause you to get lost in the details and get off track. Seeing the larger beats will help you make sense of the bigger picture. From there you can fill in the details as accurately as possible. In printed music, notes are usually arranged so that the beats are easy to see.

As you become more advanced, look for familiar patterns such as scales, arpeggios (chord outlines), familiar rhythmic groupings, and sequences. Identifying patterns will allow you to quickly grasp a measure or more at a time.

Don't Stop Now!

Use your metronome as if you are playing with a group. In other words, assume that it's not going to stop for you! Turn on your metronome, select a tempo, and play straight through the composition without stopping to fix mistakes—even notes and rhythms. The most basic skills in sight-reading are (1) staying on the

149

correct beat and (2) looking ahead. If you make a mistake, just let it go—don't look back!

You do not have to sight-read at performance tempos. Play at a tempo that you can execute as accurately as possible, maintaining the same tempo throughout. Be sure not to rush faster passages, such as sixteenth notes. This is a natural mistake to make in the heat of the moment, and will greatly reduce your accuracy.

One Thing You Can Control

Hitting all the notes is a good goal, but even when you are missing notes here and there, you should not sacrifice a consistent sound and breathing.

A good sound, besides improving the overall product, will also improve your accuracy. A missed high note is probably the result of inadequate support, not poor sight-reading!

Sight-Reading Checklist

Before You Start . . .

- Look for any really difficult passages. Finger through these passages silently.
- Tap through any difficult rhythms. At a minimum, locate the large beats and figure out how to fit the notes into them.
- Look for key and meter changes, in addition to rhythmic changes.
- Look to see if there are any repeats, including D.C. or D.S. markings at the end of the piece (see glossary); or any tempo changes.
- Know the road map before you begin.

For More Advanced Players . . .

- What is the mood of the piece? Look for dynamics and expression markings.
- What is the style of the composition? Can you identify from the composer or the title whether it is Baroque, Classical, Romantic, or Modern?
- Look to see if the piece is written for a trumpet in a specific key. If you play on a trumpet in the wrong key and fail to transpose, everything will be off.

Debrief Your Performance

Take a minute after you play to assess your performance. How was your sound quality and breathing? Did you sacrifice musicality while concentrating too much on notes and rhythms? How was your note accuracy and tuning?

For more advanced players, did you remember to play the dynamics? Did you play in the appropriate style, with all of the printed articulations? Good players can perform a piece they are reading for the first time as though they have been playing it for years.

Performance and Audition Success

Standing in front of an audience, about to perform, can be exciting. It's what we all practice to be able to do, right?

But then there are these big performances we've really been practicing for, and we wake up in the morning with butterflies in our stomach for a performance that's still twelve hours away. What is up with that?

This chapter is about the performance side of playing. It will set you up so that you are totally prepared for those big moments when it really counts, so that your experience on stage is the one that you want!

Cool under Pressure

The sensation of excitement is no different from that of anxiety. The difference lies in our thoughts and interpretation of the situation. While a little anxiety can create an exciting edge to your performance, your body may react in other ways as well—shaky or sweaty hands, increased heart rate, and shortness of breath, to name a few. These reactions can make it hard to remember and execute what you've practiced!

Alongside the physical signs of anxiety, we may begin to evaluate ourselves, feeling uncertain and losing our concentration. We may worry about getting things right. If you start to get nervous about being nervous, things can really spiral out of control, and your body will respond accordingly.

Your best bet is to notice that you are nervous and not worry about that. Let it go and return your attention to your playing. It really is possible to be relaxed when we play, if we don't get all wrapped up in our head! With the good practice and mental habits listed below, you will be able to approach each situation with calm confidence. And, of course, both performing and auditioning get easier the more often you do them. The tips below take you through the mental and physical preparation—from months ahead up to the big day itself—that will allow you to enjoy your performance as much as your audience does.

Long-Term Preparation

Rather than trying to play a piece that's beyond your current skill, choose compositions that will enhance your musical skills and strengths, so that you can spend your time polishing. Having chosen the right piece, you will get out of your performance what you put into preparation.

Your attitude as you practice will carry into your performance—and, for that matter, other areas of your life. Stay positive and motivated while practicing, always envisioning your final, polished product. Do not concentrate on impressing others; just make good music. It is exhausting to live your life constantly wondering what other people are thinking about you!

Some additional tips for thorough preparation:

- Always use a metronome. If you cannot play the entire work with a metronome, you will have a very difficult time with a piano

Healthy Mental Habits

Expecting a perfect performance every single time is unrealistic and can cause performance anxiety in any musician, amateur or professional. Don't do this to yourself—it's just another form of ego. Be modest enough to expect mistakes—they're simply a part of live performance.

Having a positive attitude throughout your life will carry over into your performance. Know what you are and are not capable of, and keep your expectations realistic.

Especially when you're challenging yourself, give yourself permission to make mistakes. When you find yourself engaging in negative self-talk (e.g., "I can't" or "what if"), refocus on more productive thoughts and attitudes instead. The thoughts that you practice will become habit, just like the music itself.

Remember that your friends and family are pulling for you and know that you have what it takes to succeed!

Preparing Audition Music

Auditioning is very similar to live performance as far as preparation, but—unlike performances—auditions are competitive! Many seasoned performers get nervous during auditions, even if they're usually cool under pressure. As with any performance, your success and confidence will reflect your preparation before the audition. If you are well prepared, you will play a great audition!

- As soon as you receive your music for an audition, be sure that any photocopied music is not cut off on the edge, missing pages, or blurry, and make sure it contains every passage listed in the audition requirements. If the music is not legible, do not hesitate to request a clean copy.
- If the music is from a larger work for an orchestra or a symphonic band, find a recording of the music to guide your preparation. Locate the passage on the CD and listen for tempo, style, dynamics, and other details. Ask your band teacher or private instructor to record the passage for you, so that you can clearly hear the trumpet line without other instruments playing.
- Begin practicing the excerpts or etudes slowly, and gradually increase the tempo once you have mastered your current tempo.
- Practice and perfect small sections before playing the whole excerpt from beginning to end.
- Work constantly with a metronome. Absolute rhythmic accuracy is a must; some judges may even tap their foot quietly while you play to check your rhythm! Once you can accurately stay with the metronome, set the metronome to "silent," to help you internalize the beat.
- Use a tuner in your practice consistently.
- Mark your music as needed, and use this to your full advantage! Always use a pencil.

accompanist, if you will be playing with one. The metronome will create reassuring stability even when you're preparing for an unaccompanied audition or performance.
- Record your playing frequently. Listen with fresh ears, as though someone else is playing, so you can hear things you would ordinarily miss while practicing.
- Plan your breaths, write them in, and follow them consistently. Nerves tend to make our breathing haphazard in performance;

"Be harder on yourself in the practice room and be easier on yourself in performance."
— Bryan Edgett

Leather and Plush: It's All about the Bags

When you get your first professional instrument, or perhaps when you get your first piccolo or C trumpet, there's no going back. Time to put that time-honored plastic case aside and treat yourself to something worthy of your new gear!

Hard Cases

Usually made from plastic or wood, hard cases are extremely durable and offer great protection for your trumpet. Most students are on the run a lot and need a case that can take a beating while protecting their trumpet.

Some models of hard cases can store multiple trumpets, but they are quite heavy. Most players who need to carry multiple instruments use a gig bag.

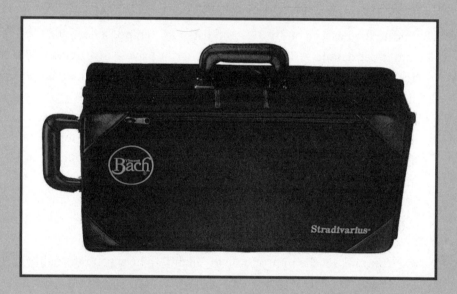

Gig Bags

These lightweight, padded bags can hold from one to five trumpets, with plenty of room for mutes, mouthpieces, and music. Available in a backpack or over-the-shoulder style, they are great for students and professionals who have to walk longer distances to class or performance venues.

Look for a bag made with good cushioning and high-quality leather or fabric. While its lighter weight is a big advantage, you should be more gentle with a gig bag than with a hard case to avoid damaging the trumpets inside.

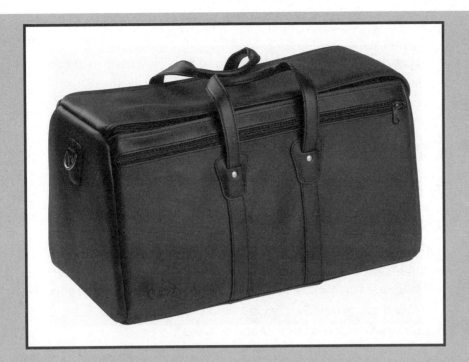

Flight Cases

These durable cases are designed to be placed in the overhead compartment of planes so that you can avoid checking your instrument as baggage. They may be available in a backpack or wheeliebag style.

Flight cases may accommodate between one and five trumpets but usually lack built-in accessory and music compartments. Many companies are now making add-ons for music and mutes, making these bags more versatile.

157

> *"Look, if you don't take the audition, you'll always wonder whether you should have, and you'll regret not taking the chance."*
>
> — Adolph "Bud" Herseth

breathe where you need to, but follow the breathing you practiced if possible.

- Set goals for each practice session, and pace yourself so that you learn your music well before the performance date. Insufficient preparation is a set-up for a stressful experience!

The Month before a Performance

- Get coaching on your music by a professional trumpeter or teacher, and from more than one person if possible.
- Focus your practice time on the spots in the music that are most difficult. The better these sound, the better the overall piece will sound.
- Make sure you are practicing exactly what is printed on the page. As we listen to ourselves, we get used to our own errors and inaccuracies. Keep your ears and eyes fresh!
- Begin each piece with a tension-free breath in the correct tempo (musicians call this "breathing in time"). This will help you change gears between pieces of different styles.
- Know whether you will play seated or standing. Different muscles are used in each case, so practice however you plan to perform.

Two Weeks before the Performance

- Reduce sugar and eliminate caffeine, to decrease your body's physical stress. (You may need to catch up on sleep when you eliminate these stimulants!)
- Practice "cuts" in the music, if there are any. Otherwise, you may forget about them under pressure.
- Practice performing each work without stopping, no matter what happens. Play multiple run-throughs each practice as you approach the performance.
- Practice breathing and self-calming techniques while visualizing the performance situation.
- Set a specific day to play a mock performance for family or friends a week or two before the actual event. If time permits, schedule separate run-throughs for several different people (director, family, and friends).
- For your mock performances, try to duplicate the atmosphere you will encounter when you perform. For example, ask your listeners to take the run-through seriously and not comment until afterward. Walk into the room and play the audition selections

> *"Whether you think you can or whether you think you can't, you're right."*
>
> — Henry Ford

from beginning to end. The more often you perform for others, the more natural it will become.

- The weekend before the performance, play three run-throughs: the first one in the morning, the second in the afternoon, and the third in the evening.

The Day before the Performance

- Avoid making changes in how you are performing the pieces. Consistency will minimize intrusive thoughts during the audition and allow you to simply play the way you've rehearsed.
- Try not to play any contact sports, or exert yourself in any way that might strain your body. Even a minor injury, soreness, or fatigue can make it difficult to perform at 100 percent.
- Get a good night's sleep for two nights before the performance. The concentration required to perform well can drain you mentally and physically.
- Do not over-practice; in fact, try to practice as little as possible the day and night before. Musicians can often be overly picky in

Calming Techniques for Performers

There are many "natural" ways to prepare yourself mentally and emotionally for a performance. Many of these ways will also help you in other nerve-wracking situations, such as public speaking or debating.

- Recall a positive performance experience and take a few minutes to visualize the sense of competence and assurance it gave you. Now, springboard those feelings into the current situation.
- Deep breathing calms the body both physically and mentally. Close your eyes and spend a few minutes slowly breathing in through your nose and out through your mouth.
- Get a massage several days before the performance so you are not sore. This will eliminate the physical tension that you hold in your muscles, along with the negativity that can accompany it.
- Bananas contain a lot of vitamin B6, which the body needs to produce serotonin, a neurotransmitter in the brain that has a calming effect. Eat a banana every day during the week of the audition. The day of the audition, eat two in the morning and another one every few hours. Don't overdo it, though—you don't want to play on a full stomach!

their practice the night before. Relax and play through what you have prepared.

- Don't clean your instrument the night before. You could drop it or injure the instrument. Plus—ironically—if you clean it you are removing particles you have become used to playing with!

- Oil your valves the night before. Don't overdo it—too much valve oil can cause a gurgling sound in the trumpet. Get all the excess water and oil out before you pack up for the night.

The Day of the Performance

- Do not eat a heavy breakfast. However, do eat! Eating will give you energy and help keep you centered and grounded. Have a couple of bananas and a piece of toast or cereal, which are easy on the stomach.

- Don't drink caffeine, which increases the body's metabolic stress (including your heart rate) for many hours.

- Make sure you pack your trumpet, mouthpiece, music, mutes, and music stand (if needed). Bring a water bottle if your mouth tends to get dry. Check that you have all your music before you leave the house; check again once you get to the car. Musicians swap stories over dinner of how they left their music sitting right by the front door, or on the music stand. Don't let that be you!

- Make sure you have warmed up well, but not so much as to create fatigue. Instead, rest your mind and body and put your visualization and calming techniques into action.

- Dress appropriately. Wear something that is nice but comfortable. Part of the audition may be behind a screen, but there may also be a time when you will interact with judges (e.g., in a final round, or after the auditions are over).

- Dress in layers so you can adjust your body temperature.

- Participants may be assigned an order or draw numbers. Have some light reading available to distract you while you wait, in case you have to wait for a long time. This is better than over-practicing or listening to everyone else practice!

- Arrive at the audition site a little early, with enough time to find the location. If you arrive late you will feel rushed. If you arrive too early you may get nervous while waiting around too long.

Read and discuss this with your parents

Performing with Beta Blockers

If you are a student who continues to be seriously affected by performance anxiety even after years of playing, and you have tried every other technique available, beta blockers can be used as a last resort. Beta blockers are prescription drugs that block the receptors that cause the symptoms of performance anxiety.

These may be appropriate if you are over eighteen, have enough performance anxiety to interfere with your playing, and have already tried other calming methods.

Since beta blockers were used originally for high blood pressure and migraines, you MUST consult a doctor for a prescription. Your body can develop a physical dependency on beta blockers if you use them too often (this should not occur if you use them only for performances). It is also possible that you have a medical condition that might make them too risky for you to use.

Possible side effects of beta blockers include asthma, headache, stomachache, and muscle cramps. For this reason, make sure you try the new medication well before the audition, on two different days, to observe your body's reaction to it. The likelihood of side effects is low if the drugs are taken in small, occasional doses.

Although I am not suggesting you use anxiety-reducing drugs, I offer this information so that you can make your own decision, with the help of your teacher, family, and doctor.

- Play your usual warm-up routine. Don't be bothered by show-offs—they may do their best playing in the warm-up room! Instead, take your time and loosen up slowly.
- Be friendly and courteous to everyone you meet. You never know who they might be or know. Don't socialize more than you're comfortable with, though. Create the space to take care of yourself and stay focused on your own priorities.
- Make sure your instrument is in working order. Check all valves and slides, and tune carefully.
- Stretch stiff or tense muscles; take slow, deep breaths.
- Expect from yourself the best that you can do. That is all anybody should ever expect from you. There's no such thing as a perfect audition!

During the Performance

- If this is a live performance (as opposed to an audition), let the audience see you are enjoying the music you are making. Be "at home" on the stage.
- Applause is the audience's way of expressing their appreciation. Smile and be gracious as you bow to acknowledge the applause.
- Trust your preparation—don't second-guess yourself! Feeling nervous is normal. It proves you are human.
- Be a part of the music you are creating. Do not worry about messing up—mistakes are a part of it. Just let them happen, and keep making music.
- Keep your bottle of water next to you, especially if your mouth gets dry while you perform. Sip the water between pieces or during a long rest.
- Gently bite the sides of your tongue for a quick bit of extra saliva.

Tips for Auditions

- The audition monitor is someone whose job is to guide the players through the audition behind the scenes. They will call you from the warm-up room, bring you to the audition room, and tell you when the judges are ready.
- When in the audition room, speak softly when you ask the proctor a question. Walk quietly to preserve the privacy and anonymity of the audition. You may be disqualified if you make yourself known to the judges, even inadvertently.
- Use your own music, if possible. There may be a copy on the stand, but ask the proctor if you can use your own, so that you're seeing familiar markings. Try to re-create your familiar environment as much as possible by adjusting your position and music stand until you are comfortable.
- Play your music in the order requested. Be prepared for anything, including additional cuts.
- Perform your music at the same tempos that you have practiced. Don't let other people auditioning influence you to make changes. Consistency is more valuable than any last-minute change.
- Take time between the audition pieces. Remember, the judges are on your time. Collect your thoughts about each excerpt before you start. If you're playing in various styles, this pause will help you get the correct mindset for each one.

"The more you play in public, the easier it is."

— Arnold Jacobs

- Keep going, even if you make a mistake! Do not stop or ask to go back. A judge may occasionally ask you to play something again. However, do not ask to play something again. Accept your performance and trust their professional judgment of your skill level.
- Do not show any reaction to what you have played. Represent yourself professionally.
- If the audition includes sight-reading, make sure you give yourself plenty of time to look over the music. Then play from beginning to end without stopping, no matter what.
- Perform confidently. The judges will be able to hear this in your sound.

After the Performance

- Pick up your materials quickly after the performance. Leave the room quietly to protect the privacy of the audition.
- Feel good about what went well in the performance or audition. If you have a recording of the performance, wait a week before listening to it.
- Accept the performance you have just given. Being positive about each performance will help you approach the next one with confidence.
- Give yourself a break. You deserve it!

Marching Band

It is both the quality of music and the precision and complexity of formations that make a marching band great. It's like an orchestra playing Beethoven's Fifth Symphony . . . while coordinating complex moving formations that weave and dance across the field.

Marching band is all about being part of something that is bigger than yourself. You will develop great friendships with everyone in the band, since you are spending many hours together—some very early in the morning and late at night! It is satisfying to be around people who are equally excited to be making music and achieving a high level of performance.

Band members get to go to all the high school football games, including regional and state playoffs, and may even travel out of state to join other bands from around the country in parades or competitions. From trips and shows to fundraisers and dinners, marching band takes a lot of organization! Students and parents share the work with the director; it is an incredible experience of teamwork as well as music-making.

School Is Out, Band Is In

Band camp takes place during a three- or four-week period during mid- to late summer and is designed to work intensively on drills, music, and show effects. It includes practices in the band room; instrumental *sectionals* (when the band breaks into individual instrumental sections, with each section led by a teacher who has experience on that specific instrument); and field practice, which begins as soon as the music is coming together and the drill is written. Some

Marching Band Jargon

Attention

Standing straight, feet together, with your body still and your instrument in a specific position.

Color Guard (or Auxiliaries)

Students who work with flags, rifles, and sabers, wearing colorful uniforms and often incorporating dance moves. Various sets of flags may be twirled, tossed, or spun. The color guard is considered part of the band (and the band class) during the fall semester, but color guard members do not sign up for band class in the spring semester unless it is to play an instrument.

Covering Down

Standing in a straight line with those in front of you, behind you, and to your left and right.

Drill

The process of moving into and out of formations; a specific series of formations.

Drill Chart

A sequence of instructions that describes a formation. A drill chart will usually include a picture showing the position of each student within the overall arrangement.

Drum Line (or Battery)

The marching portion of the percussion section; includes bass, snare and *quints* (five tenor drums mounted together).

Drum Major (or Field Commander)

Serves as student conductor on the field, leading the band on the field. If the band is large enough that sightlines are an issue, there may be three drum majors. The drum major typically conducts from the fifty-yard line, facing the band.

Drum majors of college bands may have a more showy role in performances, using a mace (long staff with an ornamented top) to conduct, and incorporating spinning and twirling routines.

Formation (or Set)

An individual image on the field; each song will contain many formations, and players are given a specific number of beats to move from one formation into the next.

Mark Time

To march in place to the beat of the music.

Pit (or Front Ensemble)

Members of the band who play on the side of the field, directly in front of the drum major. These include instruments that cannot be carried on a field, such as the timpani (kettle drum), marimba, vibraphone, and chimes. Not all percussionists stay in the pit; many are needed for the drum line (see above).

Twirlers

Baton twirlers may be added to the color guard to provide flash and movement in the show.

bands have a separate session for *rookies* (new members of the band) that meets for several days before the full camp begins.

Band camp is a chance for the entire group to bond—for established friends to spend time together and for new members to become a part of the group. After band camp is over, the band typically continues to practice each day for two or three hours either before or after school. This schedule continues throughout marching season, usually ending sometime in November.

The drum major is the student conductor of the marching band during rehearsals, performances, and competitions. With a student taking this responsibility, the director is free to view the formations, offer musical guidance, and oversee the whole performance. Bands typically hold auditions for this position in the spring semester each year.

Stripes, Uniforms, and Formations: Bands on and off the Field

Most high schools have a marching band (which doubles as a parade band for special occasions) and a smaller pep band, that consists of some members of the marching band.

Marching Band

A typical marching band consists of woodwinds, brass, percussion, and color guard (who carry flags and possibly rifles), plus the drum major, who serves as conductor. Double reed players may march on the field playing other instruments (e.g., saxophone), play in the pit, or perform with the color guard.

Marching bands typically perform at football games as halftime entertainment, and in competitive marching contests at the regional, state, and national levels. You can expect to play one show of drill and music for the entire season, constantly cleaning and fixing the drill and music so that it is brilliant and polished for each competition or performance.

Marching bands may play music of any genre, including marches, jazz, classical, Broadway musicals, rock, and film scores.

Pep Band

Performing primarily at sporting events, a pep band is really a subsection of the marching band, and is composed of woodwinds, brass, percussion, and the drum major. Pep bands do not march, but instead perform from the stands, playing music that will build excitement for the fans and athletes.

Parade Bands

Parade bands perform for celebrations such as the Thanksgiving Day Parade or the Rose Bowl, as well as ceremonies of state such as the Fourth of July. A parade band has an instrumentation similar to marching bands, sometimes adding unusual instruments such as the bagpipe or fife; and may include color guard or a baton twirler. Many military and veterans' organizations have their own parade bands.

Drum and Bugle Corps

A typical drum corps consists of the color guard, brass (no woodwinds), percussion, and the drum major, performing any style of music. Drum corps perform primarily at competitive marching contests, most notably those of Drum Corps International (DCI).

Old Guard Fife and Drum Corps

This traditional ensemble includes bugles, fifes (wooden flutes), and rope-tensioned drums. Players' uniforms are typically Revolutionary-era garb such as waistcoats, ruffled collars, and buckled shoes. The drum major directs using a ceremonial spontoon, a weapon used in the seventeenth and eighteenth centuries.

Special holiday celebrations and living-history settings may feature a fife and drum corps performing period marches.

169

Perils of the Outdoors

The sweat in our hands contains acids and oils that can eat away at the finish on a brass instrument. To keep your trumpet finish looking good, wipe it down after each rehearsal.

The only safe place to lay down your trumpet is in its case. Never place it on the pavement or grass! Bring your case with you to the field and return your trumpet to its case during breaks and at the end of rehearsal.

Protecting Yourself and Your Chops through Marching Season

To avoid performance injuries during marching season, approach your playing the same way you would in concert band. Play with a beautiful, rich sound; little tension; good breathing; appropriate dynamics; and good posture. You will especially want to maintain excellent self-care routines in terms of warm-up, warm-down, strength training, and lip care.

Here are a few things to keep in mind as you go into marching band season, to ensure that you get through the whole season in good shape!

Always warm down after practice.

It is tempting to simply pack up and race out the door after a long rehearsal or practice session. You may be mentally and physically tired and have other things to take care of, including homework. However, the next day you will find that your embouchure muscles are tight, rigid, and unresponsive. The few minutes it takes to warm down will save you time and discomfort later!

Don't play on tired lips.

Don't push your lips past their limit. If they are tired, back off your playing by using a softer dynamic and less aggressive articulations and taking high parts down an octave. Taking it easy for one rehearsal will help you avoid injuries that can require you take a much longer break from the trumpet.

If you experience pain in your embouchure as you warm up for the day, you must take that day off from playing, and you should not play again until the pain is gone. If the pain is not gone after four days, consult an experienced teacher and/or medical professional.

Be sensible about high-range playing.

If you are the lead trumpeter and you're having trouble playing the high notes, don't be afraid to request a lower part. If you want to try using a high-note mouthpiece, work with a professional trumpet player to ensure that you switch correctly between mouthpieces.

Avoid dehydration and over-hydration.

Drink enough water to avoid dehydration and heat exhaustion. But be careful: if you drink too much water, you can become sick from an imbalance of electrolytes. Alternate water with drinks that preserve your electrolyte balance.

Holiday Breaks and Summer Vacation

Holiday and summer breaks are a great time to decompress and regroup for the next semester. However, there are lots of great reasons not to put that trumpet back in your case for two solid months!

Summer vacation is time you can actually call your own. It's a relief to have fewer things going on, so you can do all the things you've been waiting to do. School can be pretty intense in terms of homework and late nights, so if you are a serious player, trumpet practice is probably high on your list.

It's easy to slide into a routine of doing nothing during the summer. Once you start your day off with a couple of hours of TV or computer games, it can be hard to break out of the pattern and actually do something that demands energy and thought!

While having a few lazy days is a welcome break, it's easy to go through the whole summer and, at the end of it, not even be able to remember how you spent all that free time. You don't have to write the next great American novel, but it would be nice to have done *something*, right?

When Chops Melt Like Ice Cream

If you are spending the breaks at home, there is no real excuse not to practice. Especially if you are a beginner, if you go two weeks without practicing over break, it will take you approximately two weeks just to get *back* to where you left off before break. Believe me, actually improving is much more exciting than getting your chops back!

You can cut your practice time in half for a few days to give yourself some downtime, but to skip practice altogether is absolutely a mistake. Make sure you put the trumpet to your face at least once a day.

Always try to bring your instrument with you when you go on vacation. If your parents tell you there's not enough room, that's fine, but do bring your mouthpiece. Mouthpiece buzzing is soft enough to not disturb anyone. If your relatives bug you about it, it's most likely because they don't understand the need to keep the muscles toned, or because they're uncomfortable with someone else being productive while they're not!

You should try to buzz for about fifteen minutes a day. If you are staying at a relative's house or a hotel, get up a little early before everyone else and buzz in the next room. Play songs you know, or make up melodies of your own; enjoy playing by ear!

Getting Your Juices Flowing

It's great to do something energetic at the beginning of your day so that even if you're just relaxing for the rest of the day, you feel positive and energized. Start the day with a sense of accomplishment and you'll have more fun with whatever else you do. Get up, eat breakfast, and get dressed . . . then go into your practice room, crack open the trumpet case, and start warming up.

Is your technique where you want it to be? Summer is a great time to start hitting the etudes, scales, and arpeggios; working on speed and clarity; building your sound; and increasing your range. Since you don't have a performance to worry about, you can focus on building technique without the distraction of quickly preparing pieces.

Kicking It Up a Notch

If you're motivated to really go somewhere with your playing, get into a professional practice routine—several practice sessions spread throughout the day.

One practice session can be spent playing along with a recording, building your ability to play by ear and improvise. Use a practice mute so you can still hear the recording while you play, or wear headphones. There are also method books for learning how to improvise, which include recordings that you can play along with.

For a fun boost, go to the music store early in the summer and pick out some interesting music, including movie music or solos you've heard. If you're someone who needs external motivation to keep you going, pick a goal such as polishing a certain piece to play for your teacher at the end of the summer.

Practicing can be as much fun as you want it to be! Or, if you prefer, it can be absolute drudgery . . . but who wants that? The point is, it's up to you. Setting goals and achieving them will keep your practice stimulating. Find the right amount of challenge for yourself—hard enough to be interesting, easy enough that you can see yourself making progress.

Summer is also a good time to take some private lessons with a great teacher that you haven't had an opportunity to study with during the year. Especially if your primary teacher leaves town for a few weeks, summer is a chance to get a new perspective on your technique or solo music.

Music on the Lawn

There are many opportunities to hear and play music during the summer that you won't have during the year. Orchestras often give free outdoor concerts during the summer, playing music that people enjoy hearing in a relaxed setting. Festivals frequently bring in national artists to perform several concerts over the summer. Don't limit yourself to just trumpet performances!

Summer music camps provide amazing opportunities to make friends and play great music. In the fall, start looking for out-of-state camps that recruit nationally. You will need to prepare and submit an audition for these programs in the early spring.

It's Your Time Now

It can be easy to forget the thrill of great music-making over the summer, without your teacher and friends around! Get into a routine early in the summer to avoid the summer slump. If you take the opportunity to inspire yourself now, you will start next year with technique to burn!

Plastic mouthpieces are sometimes used outside for cold-temperature performances, since they don't draw as much heat away from your lips. They are inexpensive and quite durable but lack the sound quality of the standard metal mouthpiece.

If you will be doing a lot of cold-weather playing, you might consider plastic or lucite rims. These rims are custom-ordered and screw onto the cup and backbore portion of a screw-rim mouthpiece. This set-up costs more than a standard mouthpiece, so a plastic mouthpiece is more economical for occasional outdoor playing.

Making Time Count

With marching band practice scheduled before or after school for two or three hours, it is important to find time to continue your private studies. You might consider asking your director if you can miss part of rehearsal one day a week to take a lesson.

You will need to be creative to fit your practice in, but it's important to continue advancing on the instrument during the fall. You can practice before school, or alternate thirty minutes of homework with thirty minutes of practicing in the evening.

Use your "down time" during the day to get a head start on your homework so you have some finished by the time you get home at night.

Returning to Concert Playing

When returning to concert playing after marching season is over, make sure you return to a normal trumpet angle. Many times the high trumpet angle from marching band carries over into the concert band playing. For concert playing your chin should be parallel to the floor or slightly tucked; your trumpet should have a slight downward tilt (see chapter 2).

Also, check your volume and make sure you're not over-playing. Trying to fill the entire stadium with your sound can be a big job. Now that you're back in the band hall, don't bury your friends with a take-no-prisoners blast!

Trumpet Care and Repair

I walk into the practice room. It is my first day teaching middle school students as part of my undergraduate degree, and Adam is my first student of the day. We make awkward introductions and he hesitantly pulls out the music he is preparing for a concert next week. He plays a passage for me; he is a capable player, but there is something odd about the sound of his cornet. Adam tells me he bought the instrument online and that it has always sounded this way. He hands me his cornet and I play a few passages; it sounds and feels strangely stuffy. In my head I write it off as yet another dealer selling inferior instruments online, but out loud I tell Adam I will clean it for him and see if it makes a difference.

During the next class period I head to the instrument storage room, fill a plastic tub with water, and submerge the trumpet. A bright object shoots out of the bell.

It is a yellow hard candy.

I finish cleaning the trumpet, reassemble it, and give the mouthpiece a twist to begin playing. When I put my lips to that cornet, the sound is unrecognizable. This is by far the best cornet I have ever played!

At the end of the year I offered to buy that cornet from Adam. He laughed and turned me down.

This chapter is about caring physically for your trumpet. The first part will show you how to clean your trumpet; the second part will give you the information you need to choose a repair person and make sure you get what you need.

Impossible to Fingerprint

Your trumpet is made out of brass, with either a clear lacquer or silver plating. The acid in our hands does not mix well with the finish on your trumpet; to keep your finish from breaking down, wipe the trumpet after each practice session with a soft T-shirt to remove the oil and acid left by your hands. Once a month, polish your instrument with a cloth designed for your specific finish, using silver polish, brass polish, or lacquer polish.

Down the Pipe

Cleaning your instrument may occasionally seem like a distraction that takes you away from your valuable practice time; but there are many parts on the trumpet, and playing well requires taking excellent care of all of them! Whether it's a yellow hard candy or dirt buildup from regular playing, any debris in your trumpet will affect tuning, resonance, and ease of playing.

Once a month you should give your trumpet a bath to clean out all the previous month's saliva deposits (acidic), food particles, and bacteria that accumulate in the trumpet each day. As you do this the first time, you will get to see the inner parts of your trumpet in detail! Removing the valves is the first step in the process. They are the most delicate part of your trumpet, so be very careful not to force anything, scratch them, or drop them.

The holes on the three valves are arranged differently to match that valve's particular slides and casing. After the trumpet bath, each valve must be returned to its own casing, facing the correct direction, for air to pass through. When a valve is inserted correctly, pressing it down causes its holes to line up with the holes in its own valve casing. To observe this for yourself, press the valve, remove the corresponding valve slide, and look into the open pipe.

To prepare to clean your trumpet, place your trumpet on your lap with the second valve slide facing you. Unscrew the top valve cap on the first valve (see page 4) and slowly pull the valve straight out. Keeping close track of which way the valve came out, examine the valve to see if its valve number is printed on it, and write down which side the number faces. Do this with each valve.

If your valves do not have numbers stamped on them, write down whether the larger or smaller side of the valve guide is facing you (see Figure 1.5, page 8) when your trumpet is resting on your lap with the second valve slide facing upward. Since the valves are not numbered, you will have to keep them in order as you bathe them so that you can reinsert them in the correct casing when you are finished.

Little Pieces of Trumpet

To prepare for your trumpet's first bath, read through all the instructions below, gather all the supplies you need, and clear some counter space in your

Trumpet Bath Supplies

- Mouthpiece brush
- Two clean, dry bath towels
- Cleaning snake
- Hand towel
- Slide grease
- Valve oil
- Cleaning cloth: large microfiber or soft cotton cloth (no paper products!)
- Valve cloth: clean microfiber cloth, cut to 7" × 16"
- Plastic flute cleaning rod, or wooden chopstick
- Liquid dish soap (minimal additives)
- Plastic tub large enough to comfortably fit your trumpet and slides

bathroom for the parts of your disassembled trumpet. Don't worry; bathing your trumpet isn't as intimidating as it seems, as long as you are organized and mind the details! Allow two hours the first time you bathe your trumpet; after a little practice you can complete the whole process in about an hour.

The supplies you will need for your trumpet bath are listed above ("Trumpet Bath Supplies"). Be sure to use only liquid soap, not detergent, to bathe your trumpet. The strong chemicals in detergent are not safe for your instrument and may damage the finish. Once you have gathered all your supplies, follow the steps below.

1. Run a lukewarm bath for your trumpet in a large plastic tub.
2. Add a moderate amount of liquid soap, just enough to make the water sudsy.
3. Place a folded bath towel next to you on a stable, level surface. The bath towel will be for the parts you are washing.
4. Place a hand towel nearby for the parts that will not be washed.
5. Remove your mouthpiece, the three valve slides (remember to depress the corresponding valve), and the tuning slide. Place them on the bath towel (Figure 17.1).
6. Remove your bottom valve caps and place them on the bath towel. These should unscrew easily. NOTE: Never use any tool to turn a stuck valve cap. Ask your teacher for help, or take the trumpet to a qualified repair person.
7. Unscrew each finger button from the valve stem. Unscrew each top valve cap and slide it over the stem.

179

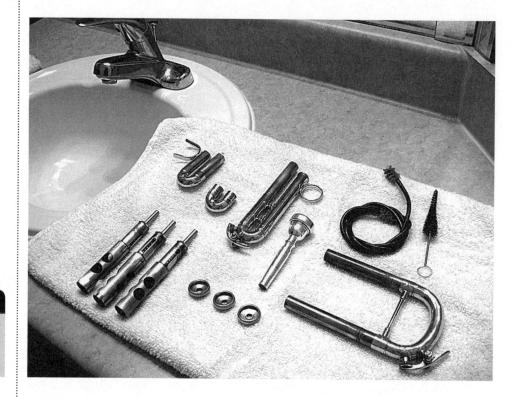

8. Place the finger buttons and top valve caps on the hand towel, keeping all of the hardware for each valve together (Figure 17.2).

9. Remove the felt pads from the valve stem and set them on the hand towel. The pads must remain dry.

10. Unscrew the nut and/or screw on the third valve slide stopper (if you have one) and carefully place it on the towel. Make sure these small parts are safe and cannot slip down the drain! (If they do get lost, though, you can get replacements at the music store.)
11. Place the valves themselves onto the bath towel.

Bubbles in the Bugle

Now that you have taken apart your trumpet and prepared the water, your trumpet is about to take a swim!

1. Place your trumpet and the contents of the bath towel into the bath. Let everything soak for 15–20 minutes to loosen dirt and deposits.
2. Run the cleaning snake or mouthpiece brush through the trumpet pipes, valve slides, and mouthpiece. Use the mouthpiece brush to gently clean the holes on the valves themselves.
3. Insert valve cloth into the eyelet of the flute cleaning rod or around a wooden chopstick, being sure to fold the cloth over the end. Dampen the cloth with warm water, insert into the valve casing and rotate to clean. The friction from pressing the valves leaves a dark residue in the casing; fold the cloth over and repeat until the cloth comes out clean.
4. Run the cleaning snake through your tuning slide, inserting from each end to ensure that all the dirt is removed. Be careful not to scratch the inner or outer surface of your trumpet with the tip of the snake.
5. Soak for five minutes to loosen any remaining deposits.
6. Drain the water out of the trumpet, by turning it. Run lukewarm water through several times to rinse out any remaining particles.
7. Drain the trumpet and carefully shake out excess water.
8. Place each cleaned piece back onto the bath towel, including the trumpet.

Rebuilding the Engine

Now that you have cleaned your trumpet, you are ready to discover if you remember how all the parts fit together! Before you reassemble the trumpet, allow it to air-dry for fifteen minutes, then dry each section of the trumpet thoroughly with a lint-free cloth. Run a clarinet swab through each pipe to eliminate any water and prevent corrosion.

Place the valves in the corresponding valve casing, facing the correct direction. Oil each one after inserting it (see page 8).

Parent supervision recommended

Giving Your Trumpet an Acid Bath

You should give your trumpet an acid bath only once a year to remove corrosion and deposits that regular cleaning is unable to remove.

In addition to the above supplies for a regular trumpet bath, you will need four gallons of vinegar and a large box of baking soda.

1. Clean your trumpet and slides thoroughly with soap and water, as described in detail in this chapter.
2. Soak all the parts for fifteen to twenty minutes in four gallons of 100 percent vinegar. Do not add water. This is the acid part of the bath.
3. Pour out the vinegar, then rinse everything thoroughly with clean water, including the tub itself.
4. Add baking soda gradually to the tub with the water running; stir constantly. If the baking soda stops dissolving, stop adding! Any undissolved baking soda will leave grit on the slides and in the trumpet.
5. Soak the trumpet and slides for fifteen to twenty minutes to neutralize the vinegar residue.
6. Thoroughly rinse your trumpet and slides in clean water.
7. Bathe the trumpet once more using soap and water. This ensures that all vinegar and baking soda deposits are removed and the trumpet is completely clean.
8. Reassemble the trumpet, applying oil and grease to the valves and slides.

Congratulations! You have just saved yourself close to $100!

Add the felt pads, screw on the top valve caps, and screw on the finger buttons and bottom valve caps.

Fasten the nut or screw onto the third valve slide (if applicable).

Apply five to six drops of valve oil to your fast (first and third valve) slides, and a bit of slide grease to the slow (second valve and tuning) slides. Insert each one into its receiver on the trumpet. Remember to depress the corresponding finger button for each valve slide before inserting it.

Insert the mouthpiece. Play a few notes to make sure everything is working correctly.

If you discover that air cannot pass through the trumpet after you replace your valves, remove your top valve caps and check to make sure each valve is in the correct casing, using the numbers printed on the valves. Then turn each valve until you hear a click and the valve is no longer free to rotate, indicating that the valve is in place. If air still cannot pass, lift the valve out of the casing and rotate it 180 degrees. You should again hear a click as the valve guide snaps into the new position.

Each time you clean your trumpet, check to see if the cork on your water key is in good condition. A worn or damaged cork can produce a buzzing sound or leaking air, affecting your trumpet's overall sound and intonation.

When You Need a Trumpet Repair

I ran into Adam several years after the candy-in-cornet incident, when I was presenting a master class to his high school band. He came up to me after the master class to chat. I reminded him of the old cornet story, and he began laughing. "You know," he said, "I should have sold you that old cornet when you offered to buy it four years ago."

"Yeah, you should have. I would have loved to play that horn," I said. I wasn't lying; I remembered that sound. "So, how is it playing these days?"

"Well, the interesting thing is, the very end of my second year in band I was waiting to go to school one morning and I had sat my cornet in its case behind my mom's car as I was helping her get my little brother in the car to go to nursery school," Adam said.

"As we backed up, we heard an unusual sound. We looked at each other, and at the same time said, 'Where is the cornet?'

"Well, my cornet was under our car and about as flat as an instrument could be that just got run over by a minivan. So, Mr. Griffin, the answer to your question about how is my cornet sounding these days—well, it's playing a little flat!"

Most instruments cannot boast as much drama in their life as that cornet had. However, every instrument needs a repair from time to time, and this section will tell you where to go and what to look for.

Dings, Dents, and Dilemmas

When first looking for someone to repair or maintain your instrument, talk to as many local professional brass musicians as you can, and find someone who specializes in brass repair. It is uncommon to find a repair person who specializes in trumpet repair; however, if you do find someone, they will tend to do the best work. You will generally find that there is one repair person in town that everybody recommends.

Before handing over your trumpet, try to look over some work they did on someone else's instrument. This will give you a good idea of their skill and attention to detail. Don't limit yourself to just one repair; the more work you see, the more accurate your assessment will be. A good, professional repair should leave minimal ripples or scarring in the metal.

When possible, take your trumpet to locally owned repair shops rather than national chains. Individual craftspeople and local businesses are motivated to provide high-quality, personal service because their reputation in the music community depends on it.

Dents to Dollars

As far as price is concerned, know that each repair job is different. There is an unpredictable element to any damage, so a reputable repair person usually will not give you an estimate by simply looking at the instrument. They will instead take their time inspecting the trumpet, looking for any problems that may arise during the course of repair.

Let the repair person know that you would like a price quote, and ask for the lowest and highest estimates possible, based on the amount of time he or she thinks will be required. Use this price range to help you make your decision. Remember that the best price may not indicate the best repair.

Masters of the Metal

There are a few legendary repair persons spread throughout the country whose work is well known among brass players. If your trumpet is of professional quality and has a significant dent or needs major valve work, this is the time to bring in a master. The top trumpet professionals in your area will know who these folks are and can give you their contact information.

Assuming that you do not happen to live close to the repair person, you will have to ship your trumpet, then wait for your instrument to be repaired in the order it was received. This may take anywhere from two weeks to six months. For a specialized repair, though, you will get what you pay for, and it is worth the wait!

18

Musical Destinations

My dad's trumpets never got much time in the case.

Just off the kitchen, our little dining room was littered with trumpets—a piccolo on the table, a B♭ trumpet on the rug, and mouthpieces everywhere. Between meat, potatoes, and five or six trumpets of various shapes and sizes, my dad's needs were met.

The flugelhorn was his favorite. Sometimes I would see him walk into the kitchen, pause, and turn back to the door of the music room, where the flugelhorn rested, waiting for him. He would look around to see if anyone was watching, then go in and play a few notes—just enough to reconnect.

He spent his days as a highly successful engineer, but where he came to life was on stage at night, with band members to his right and left, a drum set behind, and cases thrown open on the floor. My mom was always there, seated at a table with a drink and a smile, listening to songs she'd heard a hundred times and still loved because he was playing them. It was a world of dancing and laughing, longtime friends who knew each other like family. It wasn't his career; it was his passion.

When I began telling people I wanted to play the trumpet for a living, I got many different responses. For some people, it reminded them of their own desire to pursue their passion as a career. They would sigh and tell me how great it was for me to make a living doing what I loved.

Others were convinced it was the beginning of a solitary, desolate existence of poverty and struggle. I should do something "real" for a living; something secure—a safe, normal job—and play trumpet as a hobby.

"Music is your own experience, your thoughts, your wisdom. If you don't live it, it won't come out of your horn."

— Charlie Parker

185

As I entered college, I didn't know if I would succeed. I couldn't guarantee that I would be good enough to beat fifty other trumpeters to win a job in an orchestra, or convince a dignified college interview board that I was more qualified than all the other applicants.

All I knew was . . . I wanted to play trumpet.

While some portions of this chapter are intended as a road map for the young adult trumpeter, as a whole this chapter is for students anywhere in their artistic journey. Whoever you are, and wherever you are going, I acknowledge you for the dedication that got you here, and wish you fulfillment as you find your unique path.

Through Frustration, Achievement

Whenever you begin something new, it goes without saying that . . . you can't do it yet.

Yet somehow, it always comes as a surprise when, learning a new skill, we discover we are unskillful, awkward, and can't make things work. From playing the trumpet to building model airplanes, we want things to work well *now*.

Or certainly by the end of the month, right?

It's only human to react when a challenge comes up. You might get frustrated with your teacher or yourself, blame whoever thought it was a good idea for you to play the trumpet, and tell yourself that you're too busy, untalented, or dense. You begin practicing less and less. Underneath it all, you are upset and stuck, and your progress stalls.

Whenever you get into a negative spiral, deep down you know it, and there is a sense of having failed to break through your own barriers. You might walk away from the trumpet in frustration now, but the next time you face a challenge, that old failure is still sitting there, covered in dust and cobwebs but smelling freshly of the old disappointment.

Give the trumpet everything you've got. Fall in love; go past your own limits. The only path to achievement is through failure; there is no way around. Don't give yourself permission to get discouraged; it's an indulgence that lets you off the hook for giving whatever it would take. Remember why you're doing it in the first place, and find the tenacity to push through until you get where you're going.

If there are talented people around you that you admire, use them as a source of positive inspiration, but don't spend time making yourself feel bad for not playing as well as they do. Everyone learns at their own pace. Until you decide that you're fine with that, you will always be at the mercy of whatever situation you find yourself in. Keep your own goals and standards, and use competition to motivate you, not to put yourself down.

Bring the Horn to the Bull

Take advantage of private lessons, listening opportunities, and concerts or shows you can attend. Listen to recordings, and always have in mind the next several pieces you want to play! Don't be shy to talk to people about what you're working on or learning. You will learn just by putting yourself in these conversations and being open to interesting new information.

If you are in school, there may be a district or regional band event that students can audition for each year. The players who are selected rehearse for a week and perform a single concert, for an intense, fun week with some of the best players in your geographic area, all performing challenging music together. Many school districts also sponsor a solo and ensemble festival. This is an opportunity to perform for a professional musician who will give you supportive and constructive comments about your playing and give you a score that gives you a sense of your progress in relation to other players.

Music is everywhere, and amateurs of every age and ability can find opportunities to play in community bands and orchestras, brass quintets, casual backyard get-togethers, Latin bands, Renaissance or early music ensembles, religious services, and more. If you haven't found an opportunity that matches your interests, talk to the musicians you know and use online social-networking sites to connect with other people who want to create the same thing.

Music is part of the fabric that connects people; there is something timeless and unique about the kinship created in an evening of music with friends.

Leading with Your Bell

If you are considering studying music in college, take every opportunity to participate in master classes, summer programs, and additional ensemble experiences. Use your teacher as a sounding board as you make decisions about what professional direction to take, and involve them in your college research as much as possible.

Don't be shy to ask your teachers for their advice; they may not offer advice unless you ask, but if you do, they will be happy to share their insights and help you avoid making the mistakes they made. They can also use their reputation and contacts to open doors that might be closed to you. A single call from your director to their old college buddy could change the entire course of your career. It is worth asking!

If you play a wicked trumpet, there are many colleges that will give you a generous scholarship to study at their school—even if your grades in the rest of your classes are lower than you might wish. Don't assume that you can't go to your dream school! You don't know until you try. Apply to the colleges with programs that excite you, play a great audition, and let them decide.

There are many opportunities to play trumpet in college, even if you don't plan to major in music. Use your elective hours to play in an ensemble for non-majors, study privately, and take music appreciation or improvisation classes that will open up new worlds in your musical journey.

Twelve Notes, More Careers

There are four main avenues open to students pursuing a career in music, and many jobs within these broad areas: (1) performance, (2) education, (3) arts management, and (4) sound engineering (including recording). If you are interested in pursuing music as a career, you should explore each of these options to decide which one best suits your personality and skills.

If you choose trumpet performance, consider whether you're most interested in being a soloist, orchestral musician, chamber musician, band musician (jazz, Latin, etc.), commercial musician (film and studio recording), or college professor. Many players combine several of these, increasing their earning ability and keeping them balanced and challenged.

If you love performing, your focus should be finding a school with a respected performance degree, and a trumpet professor you connect with both personally and professionally. When you are planning your college visits, schedule a lesson with the prospective teacher, or arrange to observe another student's lesson or a master class. Your professor will be guiding you as you begin to shape your career; it is important that you have good chemistry with them, and that they can give you the training you are paying for in both time and money!

Your best investment in your career is choosing the right school for the right reasons. The more intelligently you research your choice, examining your options and seeking every possible opportunity, the more likely you will find the school (and professor) that is a perfect fit for you.

Wielding the Mighty Stick

My friend Samantha wasn't the most outgoing person in the band, or the most brilliant player. Few people knew her outside the band, and even within the band she didn't draw much attention. A clarinetist, she was soft-spoken but always prepared.

You could not find someone who had a bad thing to say about Samantha. She was everyone's best friend, and the band director relied on her to get things done. Although Samantha was seemingly overshadowed by players who were wittier and more outspoken, her quiet assurance somehow set the tone for the whole band. It would have been a different place without her.

Five years after we had all graduated high school, I returned to visit my parents over Christmas and learned that Samantha was the band director for the middle school in her own home town, thirty minutes away. It made all the sense in the world—she had been the heart of our band. Standing in front of it was the natural place for her.

Excellence on the Podium

There are few more exciting things than giving students one of the most memorable experiences of their lives. Having a symphony of sound at the end of your baton is an extraordinary sensation as well! If you are pursuing music education, look for a program that provides opportunities for you to develop as both a player and a teacher—one that is up-to-date and energized about new ideas in music education, and that offers a wide range of experiences for you to pass on to your students.

With your teacher's help, research which universities have an excellent and diverse music education program and a high job-placement rate. Start to think about how much trumpet playing you still want to be doing during your education degree. If you love playing and want to continue being challenged at the highest level, choose a school whose performance and education programs are well-coordinated in addition to being strong individually. The more highly developed you are as a performer, the more artistry and experience you will bring to your students in the classroom.

Even if you're majoring in education, arrange a meeting with the trumpet teacher at each school you are considering. Make sure you respect their playing, and also ask them about their teaching philosophy and experience. You are looking for a teacher who is a model of excellent teaching and playing, whether or not they have an impressive solo resume.

Beyond the Last Page

Why play trumpet?

Each person has his or her own answer to this question—sometimes the answer even changes from one day to the next, or from one hour to the next.

Some days I am playing because I love getting swept away in the sound of the orchestra, being part of a hundred people giving themselves over into some indescribable unity of sound moving through time. Other days it's because I love the challenge of lining up notes with mathematical precision, hearing the rhythms of each orchestral part weave together like the most fantastic mechanical clockwork.

Some afternoons the Arutunian *Trumpet Concerto* may hang like mist in my practice room, its slow movement sweet and sensual, its harmonies ebbing and flowing, etched with gypsy-like whimsy. Other days it may be the first movement of Mahler's fifth symphony—its insistent and foreboding fanfare yielding to sad sweetness, working into a frenzy, then subsiding into exhaustion.

At the end of a long day, I walk in the door of my house, throw on a recording of Miles Davis at full volume, and let the jazz wash the dullness from my soul. When I'm depressed and can't bring myself to even open the case, I turn on a recording of a Tchaikovsky's Fourth Symphony or Stravinsky's Rite of Spring; their throbbing passion and vitality bring me to to life again.

Watch a video recording of Doc Severinsen. Do it today, not tomorrow; life is short, and the imagination cannot compare. Eyes closed in extreme concentration, perspiration on his forehead, lips flat against the mouthpiece, notes flying at lightning speed, his playing shakes us awake and reminds us that all of us are capable of far more than we ever thought possible.

As you look at him standing on stage, know that who he is, you are. You could not be stunned and moved by such exquisite mastery if it were not part of your own fabric.

Over a lifetime, each of us has experienced moments when it seems that who we are is something extraordinary, if someone would just show us the way. It is as though the curtain of ordinariness has parted for just a moment.

Then the curtain falls closed. We forget what we saw. Months or even years may go by. But it is impossible to forget the truth of such moments.

If you have allowed the curtain of ordinariness to fall over your life—even just a little—my invitation to you is to gently move it to the side, and let your life be given by that dream.

This book is here to help you put the foundation under it.

Timeline

Prehistory

Conch shells, bones, and other natural items were used to amplify the human voice. The Jewish *shofar* is made from a ram's horn and enjoys a ceremonial use today.

1066–1485 AD

An ancient Tibetan trumpet was called the *Rkang-gling.* "Rkang" means leg-bone; the instrument was made from a human femur.

1614

Cesare Bendinelli's *Tutta l'arte della Trombetta,* is written, including tonguing exercises and ensemble pieces.

1678

Giovanni Bonaventura Viviani publishes *Two Sonatas for Trumpet and Organ,* the earliest known work for organ with trumpet solo.

c. 1750–1815

The trumpet is integrated into orchestral playing during the Classical Period

BC

Moses gives two silver trumpets to the priests.

450 BC

Greeks use the trumpet primarily for military purposes; it is made of ivory with a bronze bell.

1390–1400 AD

Trumpet makers learn to bend metal tubing, allowing them to make trumpets in an "S" shape.

1500s

Nuremburg, Germany becomes the center of trumpet making.

1623

Imperial Guild of Trumpeters and Kettledrummers is formed

b. 1662

John Shore— Trumpeter for Henry Purcell.

b. 1707

Valentine Snow— George Frederick Handel's trumpeter in England

1352 BC

Silver and bronze trumpets are placed in the burial tomb of the Egyptian King Tutankhamun.

1413

Earliest illustration of looped trumpet, in *Book of Hours of the Duke of Berry*

1638

Girolomo Fantini's *Modo per imperare a sonare di tromba* becomes the first published trumpet method book.

Timeline

b. 1766 — Anton Weidinger—Trumpeter, premiered the Haydn and Hummel trumpet concertos

1793 — Keyed trumpet developed by Anton Weidinger.

1795 — Johann Ernst Altenburg writes *Trumpeters' and Kettledrummers' Art*, discussing the historical and contemporary practices of trumpet playing.

1800 — Haydn's trumpet concerto is premiered by Anton Weidinger.

1804 — Hummel's trumpet concerto is premiered by Anton Weidinger.

1810 — The keyed bugle is invented by adding keys to an 18th century field bugle.

1818 — Heinrich Stölzel and Friedrich Blumel patent an early version of the piston valve.

b. 1825 — Jean-Baptiste Arban—First performing cornet soloist

1826 — Hector Berlioz is the first composer to use a valved cornet in an orchestral work, *Les francs-juges.*

1827 — Josef Kail commissions the earliest known work for solo valve trumpet.

1829 — Etienne-François Périnet files a French patent on the three valve cornet.

1831 — Valves are added to the German posthorn, making the first cornet.

1832 — The rotary valve is invented by Joseph F. Riedl in Vienna.

1839 — Etienne- François Périnet invents today's modern valve, or Périnet valve.

1840 — The F and G valved trumpets become the standard for orchestral performing, replacing natural trumpets.

1840 — Valves are substituted for keys to create a valved flugelhorn.

1842 — New York Philharmonic founded

c. 1860 — François Millereau builds the first piccolo sopranino trumpet, with two valves and in the key of B♭.

A Timeline for the Trumpet

1862 — General Butterfield writes "Taps," a variation of a traditional bugle call of French origin, to honor his troops after the Seven Days battle of the Civil War.

1864 — Jean-Baptiste Arban publishes *Grand Method for Cornet.*

b. 1867 — Hebert L. Clarke—Cornet virtuoso

1870 — The Bb trumpet becomes the instrument of choice by orchestral trumpet players in Germany due to improved accuracy and projection over the F

b. 1873 — Max Schlossberg, in Eastern Europe; leading American trumpet pedagogue

1875 — C. G. Conn, a musical instrument company, is founded.

1880 — F. Besson Paris produces the first trumpet in C; this will become the standard for orchestral playing.

1881 — Boston Symphony Orchestra

1882 — Berlin Philharmonic Orchestra

1885 — The first G piccolo trumpet is built by F. Besson, in Paris.

1891 — Chicago Symphony Orchestra

1892 — John Philip Sousa Band

1893 — Hebert L. Clarke joins the John Philip Sousa Band as the solo cornetist.

1893 — First trumpet produced by King Musical Instrument Company.

1900 — Dallas Symphony Orchestra

1900 — The Philadelphia Orchestra

b. 1901 — Louis Armstrong—Jazz trumpeter and singer

1902 — Max Schlossberg arrives in New York

1904 — London Symphony Orchestra

1905 — Franz Alexander builds a piccolo trumpet for A. Goeyens to perform Bach's *Brandenburg Concerto No. 2.*

1911 — San Francisco Symphony

1913 — Houston Symphony Orchestra

1916 — Vincent Bach begins making trumpet mouthpieces.

1918 — Goldman Band

b. 1921 — Adolph "Bud" Herseth—Principal trumpet of Chicago Symphony for 53 years

1922 — Two Egyptian trumpets found in Tutankhamun's tomb.

b. 1925 — Armando Ghitalla—Principal trumpet with the Boston Symphony Orchestra for 28 years

b. 1926 — Miles Davis—Jazz trumpeter

1905 — Belgian trumpet maker Victor Mahillon produces the first three-valve piccolo trumpet.

b. 1906 — Rafael Mendez—Mexican trumpet soloist

b. 1912 — William Vacchiano—Soloist, teacher at Juilliard for 67 years.

b. 1916 — Harry James—Big band soloist

b. 1917 — Dizzy Gillespie—lead trumpeter in developing bebop

b. 1919 — Roger Voisin—Soloist, on Tanglewood Music Center faculty for 68 years

b. 1921 — Timofei Dokshitzer—Russian trumpeter; composed the cadenza to Arutunian's Trumpet Concerto

1923 — Louis Armstrong performs his first recorded solo, *Chimes Blues,* with King Oliver's band.

1926 — Vincent Bach begins manufacturing trumpets

1927 — Schilke begins making trumpet mouthpieces.

1951 — Armando Ghitalla is appointed to Boston Symphony Orchestra; he will serve as principal trumpet

1949 — Robert Giardinelli, mouthpiece maker, opens shop in New York.

1946 — First full recording of the Haydn's trumpet concerto by Harry Mortimer.

1947 — First trumpet produced by Getzen Company.

1944 — Dizzy Gillespie records "A Night in Tunisia."

1935 — Eldon Benge, a renowned custom builder in Chicago, begins making trumpets.

1932 — First recording of Bach's *Brandenburg Concerto No. 2* by Paul Sporri.

b. 1933 — Maurice Andre—Made over 300 recordings; his transcriptions are the core of modern piccolo trumpet repertoire

b. 1928 — Maynard Ferguson—Famous for his extreme high-range playing in a pop jazz style.

1951 — Philip Jones Brass Ensemble

b. 1950 — David Hickman—Trumpet virtuoso and brass pedagogue

1948 — Adolph "Bud" Herseth is appointed principal trumpet, Chicago Symphony Orchestra, where he will serve 53 years.

1946 — The famous Theo Charlier etude book, *Trente-Six Études Transcendantes*, is published in France.

1945 — Timofei Dokshitzer is appointed to Bolshoi Theater Orchestra, where he will serve until 1983.

b. 1936 — Edward H. Tarr—Created a groundswell of interest in the performance of Baroque trumpet.

1935 — Walter Holy begins Baroque trumpet revival performing on a Steinkopf-Finke reproduction.

b. 1933 — Joan Hinde, female British trumpeter, who won over 50 competitions by the age of 12

1930 — The British music publishing company Boosey & Hawkes is established.

b. 1927 — Carl "Doc" Severinsen—Bandleader and trumpet soloist of the "Tonight Show Band"

Timeline

- **b. 1952** — Allen Vizzutti—Dazzling virtuoso, author of a multi-volume trumpet method
- **b. 1953** — Philip Smith—Principal trumpet of the New York Philharmonic
- **b. 1961** — Håkan Hardenberger—Soloist, commissioned many new works for trumpet
- **b. 1964** — Wynton Marsalis—Classical and jazz trumpet artist and the first jazz musician to be awarded a Pulitzer Prize
- **b. 1969** — Niklas Eklund—Baroque trumpet specialist and recording artist
- **1973** — Susan Slaughter became the first woman to serve as Principal Trumpet in a major symphony
- **b. 1977** — Sergei Nakariakov—Trumpet prodigy, began his recording career at the age of 15

- **1964** — The St. Louis Brass Quintet
- **1966** — Yamaha hires Renold Schilke as a brass consultant.
- **1971** — Empire Brass Quintet
- **b. 1978** — Alison Balsom, award-winning British soloist

- **1956** — Renold Schilke begins manufacturing trumpets.
- **1964** — Marie Speziale became the first woman trumpeter in a major symphony orchestra
- **1968** — Louis Armstrong records *"What a Wonderful World"*
- **1970** — The Canadian Brass
- **1972** — Drum Corps International
- **1974** — German Brass

- **1953** — A dancer falls on Dizzy Gillespie's trumpet and bends the bell upward 45 degrees; this becomes Gillespie's trademark.
- **1963–1964** — Armando Ghitalla makes the first recording of the Hummel trumpet concerto.
- **1966** — Renold Schilke begins producing piccolo trumpets; his model will become the American standard.

Christopher Martin wins principal trumpet of Chicago Symphony Orchestra at the age of 29.

2005

Trumpet Museum, Bad Sackingen, Germany, is established under Edward Tarr.

1985

David Monette makes his first mouthpieces.

1985

Friedemann Immer makes the first ever recording of the Haydn trumpet concerto on a period instrument.

1987

Summit Brass Ensemble

1985

Dallas Brass Quintet

1983

Wynton Marsalis becomes first artist ever to win a Grammy for classical and jazz in the same year.

1984

David Monette begins building trumpets.

1983

Additional
Resources

Glossary

A cappella — without accompaniment

A piacere — at pleasure, not strictly in tempo

A tempo — at the previous tempo

Accelerando — getting faster

Accidental — sharp, flat, or natural which appears in the middle of the piece to alter a note. Applies until the end of the measure, and only to notes in that particular octave.

Acoustic — playing without amplification

Ad libitum — at liberty, freely

Adagietto — slightly faster than adagio

Adagio — slow, leisurely

Agevole — lightly

Agitato — agitated

Al Coda — to the coda

Al Fine — to the end

Alla — in the style of; literally, "to the"

Allegretto — moderately fast, between andante and allegro

Allegro — lively, fast, brisk

Andante — "walking pace"; moderately slow

Andantino — a little quicker than andante

Animando — getting faster

Aria — lyrical song for solo voice, with instrumental accompaniment

Arpeggio — notes of a chord played one after the other

Articulation — a description of how separated or connected the notes are

Assai — fairly, quite

Attacca — going on to the next section or movement without a pause

Ballad — a song that tells a story

Ballet — dance set to music that depicts a story

Bar — regular division in music, in which the strongest beat is usually considered the first beat of each bar

Baritone — male singing voice that is between bass and tenor

Barline — vertical line separating two measures or bars

Baroque — period of musical history circa 1685–1750. Bach and Handel composed during this time.

Baton — stick used by the conductor to show the beat

Blues — type of American music derived from spirituals and work songs, characterized by "blue" notes and 12 bar chord sequence

Bore — inside diameter of a tube

Bravura — boldness

Bugle — valveless brass instrument that plays only the notes of the overtone series

Cadenza — in a work for solo and orchestra, a virtuosic passage which the soloist plays alone

Calando	gradually getting slower and/or softer	**Decrescendo**	getting softer
Cantabile	lyrical, in a singing style	**Diminuendo**	getting softer; diminishing
Chord	three or more notes played at once, usually arranged in a triad	**Dolce**	sweetly
		Double flat	(♭♭), lowers the pitch two half-steps
Chromatic	ascending or descending by half steps	**Double sharp**	(𝄪), raises the pitch two half-steps
Coda	short passage ending a movement	**Downbeat**	first beat of the bar; usually receives the strongest emphasis
Comodo	comfortable; easy (in tempo)		
Con	with	**Elegy**	instrumental lament for the dead
Con Brio	with spirit	**Enharmonic**	two notes are "enharmonically equivalent" if they have different names but sound the same; for example, A♭ and G♯
Con Fuoco	with fire		
Con grazia	gracefully		
Con leggerezza	lightly		
Con moto	with motion; moving ahead	**Espressivo**	expressively
Con sordino	with mute	**Etude**	a musical study, practice piece
Con tutta forza	with all force	**Excerpt**	short section taken from a larger composition
Concert pitch	the sounding note of an instrument, in non-transposing terms	**Fantasia**	a piece writtten freely, without using a pre-established form
Concerto	work for soloist and orchestra, usually in three movements	**Fermata**	long hold on a note or rest
Consort	17th-century term for instrumental chamber ensembles, or a composition written for a consort	**Fine**	"end"; signals the end of the piece
		Flexibility	in trumpet terms, the ability to use the lips to move from note to note
Corno da caccia	"hunting horn"; shaped similar to a French horn but higher in pitch, the corno da caccia was a popular solo instrument during the 18th century	**Forte**	(𝆑) loud
		Fortissimo	(𝆑𝆑) very loud
		Fuoco	fire and energy
		Giocoso	playfully
Crescendo	getting louder	**Glissando**	sliding smoothly and gradually between notes
Da capo al fine (D.C. al fine)	going back to the beginning and playing to the word "Fine"		
		Grandioso	majestically
Dal segno al fine	going back to the sign 𝄋 and playing to the word "Fine"	**Grave**	slow, serious

Grazia, con	with grace	**Medley**	quotes from different works combined into one continuous work
Half step	smallest distance between two pitches. On the piano, each white key to the neighboring black key is a half step.	**Meno**	less
		Meno mosso	more slowly ("less moving")
		Mezzo forte	(*mf*) medium loud
Harmony	two or more notes played at the same time to create a desired sound	**Mezzo piano**	(*mp*) medium soft
		Minuet	Baroque dance in triple meter and a moderate speed
Intermezzo	piece played between acts of an opera or ballet; a work in this style	**Moderato**	moderately fast
		Molto	very
Interval	the distance between two notes	**Morendo**	dying away
Key	set of pitch relationships in which one note is considered the resting note and other notes lead to or away from this note	**Opus**	number identifying at what point in a composer's career a piece was written
		Ossia	"or"; indicates an alternate way to play a passage
Key signature	an indication at the beginning of a piece of all the sharps or flats to be played.	**Ottava alta**	octave higher, 8va
		Ottava bassa	octave lower, 8^{ba}
Larghetto	a little faster than largo	**Overtones**	higher notes produced by a fundamental tone, as a result of the vibration of small sections of a string or column of air
Largo	very slow		
Legato	connected, no space between notes		
Leggiero	light	**Overture**	introductory music for an opera, oratorio or ballet
Lento	slow		
L'istesso tempo	the same tempo	**Partita**	suite of Baroque dances
Lunga	long	**Pesante**	heavy, rough
Lyrical	vocal in quality	**Phrase**	a division or section of a musical line
Maestoso	majestic		
Marcato	marked; short and emphatic	**Pianissimo**	(*pp*) very soft
Marcia	march	**Piano**	(*p*) softly
Marciale	march-like	**Più**	more
Measure	regular grouping of notes into a specific number of beats, separated by barlines. Also, "bar."	**Più mosso**	faster
		Poco a poco	little by little
		Poco più	a little faster

Polka	a dance in duple meter, originating in Bohemia and very popular in the 19th century	**Simile**	continue in the same way
		Slur	curved line over two or more notes, indicating that they should be played smooth and connected
Portamento	mild glissando between two notes for an expressive effect		
		Solo	passage or work for one performer; plural *soli*
Premiere	first performance of a piece of music	**Sonata**	piece for two instruments, usually in four movements, with related thematic material in a specific form
Prestissimo	very rapidly		
Presto	very fast		
Primo	first	**Sostenuto**	sustained; in a slower tempo
Quasi	nearly, almost	**Sotto voce**	in subdued style
Rallentando	slower and slower	**Staccato**	short and separated
Recitative	form of singing or playing modeled on speech, rhythmically free	**Strepitoso**	noisy, boisterous
		Stretto	pressed together; getting faster
Repeat	a musical sign that indicates a section of music should be played again	**Stringendo**	getting faster
		Subito	suddenly
		Symphony	piece for large orchestra, usually in four movements
Reprise	refrain; section of music that returns	**Syncopation**	the placing an accent on a weak beat
Risoluto	resolute, decisive		
Ritardando (rit.)	slowing down gradually	**Tacet**	direction not to play a portion of the music
Ritenuto	held back		
Rubato	literally, "borrowed"; with flexible tempo	**Tema**	theme
		Tempo	speed of a musical passage, measured in beats per minute
Scherzo	joke; movement in a quick tempo		
Semplice	simple, plain, pure	**Tempo giusto**	in exact tempo
Sempre	always	**Tempo primo**	original tempo
Senza	without	**Tendonitis (tendinitis)**	inflammation of the muscles or tendons, resulting from injury or overuse
Sforzando	(*sfz*) sudden strong accent	**Tenuto**	held, sustained
Sight read	play a piece of music you have never seen before	**Tessitura**	range of an instrumental or vocal part

Tie	curved line the connects two notes with the same pitch, combining their note values into one longer note	**Valve**	device on brass instruments that allow the instrument to play chromatically by increasing or decreasing the length of tubing
Timbre	sound color; rhymes with "amber"	**Vibrato**	regular, small variation in pitch to add warmth to the sound
Transpose	play a musical passage higher or lower than the printed key	**Virtuoso**	a performer with superb technical ability
Tremolo	trembling, quivering effect		
Triad	three notes separated by notes in between, for example A, C, E	**Vivace**	lively tempo
		Vivo	brisk, quick
Troppo	too much	**Vocalise**	vocal piece sung to vowels only, without consonants; used to develop sound and flow between notes
Tutti	all		
Unison	two or more performers sounding the same note or melody line		
		Whole step	equal to two half steps; the first step of any major or minor scale
Upbeat	second half of the beat, which leads into the downbeat		
Valse	waltz; dance in triple time, with the accent on the first beat		

Famous Trumpeters
You Should Know

The trumpeters and ensembles below reflect a wide range of musical styles, and you'll hear their names among professionals and during your studies. Seek out recordings of these players and get to know their individual styles.

Lunch with Wynton Marsalis

An incredible legacy from the great performers of the past, recordings offer an immediate and intimate experience of the playing of famous trumpeters. Notes and phrases are caught in time and captured forever, offering you a personal relationship with the great artists who reached their peak before you were born. Growing up with technology at your fingertips, it's easy to forget what a miracle it is to have the New York Philharmonic or Wynton Marsalis piping through your earbuds, available for a private performance whenever you choose!

If you have a genre you already prefer (jazz, mariachi, or classical, for example), keep your ears open to other styles, and attend as many live concerts as you can. As a musician you will want to know and respect various styles besides the one you are most comfortable playing.

If you immerse yourself in the musical seascape of world-class artists, you will gradually begin to listen to your own playing in a more sophisticated way. You will notice where your playing already has polish and finesse, and you will work until every note is at that level. As you develop your skill on the trumpet and continue discovering music, don't forget the other side of music-making! Sit in an audience and listen to great musicians perform live. Great performers communicate with every movement of their body, giving the music a visceral excitement. You'll want to rush home and practice!

Maurice Andre	French miner's son who pioneered the trumpet as a solo instrument, with virtuosic playing and transcriptions of violin and other concertos. Made hundreds of recordings; equally influential as an educator.
Louis Armstrong	Went from a New Orleans street corner to become the first famous jazz and blues trumpeter. His albums include *Ding Dong Daddy* and *Potato Head Blues*. Invented the "scat" style of singing with nonsense syllables.
Eric Aubier	French soloist and educator and student of Maurice Andre. Has recorded more than 70 works in various styles, including many premieres.
Blast	This innovative group took outdoor drum and bugle corps performances to the concert stage, with elements of theater, including props, lighting, costumes, and demanding choreography.
Canadian Brass	Recording more than 60 CDs, this group lit up concert stages worldwide with their serious and comedic presentations of classical chamber works for brass. Their commissions and arrangements are a cornerstone of the brass chamber music repertoire.

Bill Chase	Trumpeter best known for his fusion of rock and jazz into his band, called Chase. His crystal-clear, accurate, extreme high-range playing helped make him famous as the lead trumpet in Woody Herman's Thundering Herd during the 1960s.
Vincent Cichowicz	Former member of the Chicago Symphony Orchestra and professor at Northwestern University; a founding member of the International Trumpet Guild.
Herbert L. Clarke	Clarke gained national fame playing with John Philip Sousa's band beginning in 1893. His later career included conducting and writing cornet solos and four method books.
Ray Crisara	As a professor at the University of Texas, Crisara was one of the great teachers of the twentieth century. His performing career included positions with the NBC Symphony Orchestra and the Goldman Band.
Miles Davis	Shaped jazz through his innovative playing and composing, including new harmonies and electronic music. Several of his pieces are now jazz standards.
Timofei Dokshitzer	Russian trumpeter, soloist, and principal trumpet with Bolshoi Theatre.
Niklas Eklund	Best known for his Baroque trumpet performances of works from that era.
Empire Brass	Led by trumpet virtuoso Rolf Smedvig, Empire is one of the premier brass ensembles in the country, performing in the same era as the Canadian Brass.
Jon Faddis	Student and friend of Dizzy Gillespie, this preeminent jazz performer and conductor has performed on albums with such famous singers as Eric Clapton, Aretha Franklin, Billy Joel, Quincy Jones, and Tina Turner.
Maynard Ferguson	Big-band leader and jazz trumpeter with more than 60 albums to his name; instrument designer, record producer, composer, arranger, producer of film soundtracks, dedicated teacher, and three-time Grammy award nominee.
Armando Ghitalla	Important pedagogue and orchestra player in Boston and Houston. He taught many of the virtuosi of the next generation at music schools throughout the country.
"Dizzy" Gillespie	Jazz trumpeter and an architect of the jazz "bebop" movement; his "Groovin' High," "A Night in Tunisia," and "Manteca" are jazz classics.
Ludwig Guttler	German trumpet soloist, conductor, and scholar especially interested in works for *corno da caccia*.
Hakan Hardenberger	Swedish soloist who has performed with practically every major symphony.
Adolph "Bud" Herseth	Legendary principal trumpeter of the Chicago Symphony; served in the position for 53 years.

Harry James	Jazz trumpeter who played with the Benny Goodman orchestra and then led his own group; more than 75 top-twenty hits.
Chuck Mangione	A trumpeter best known in the jazz world for performing on the flugelhorn. He is most well known for his tune "Feels So Good."
Wynton Marsalis	Winner of multiple Grammy awards for his jazz and classical performances; Pulitzer Prize winner for his original compositions for brass, string quartet, and ballet.
Ray Mase	Trumpeter of the American Brass Quintet, solo recording artist, and head of the brass department at the Juilliard School of Music.
Rafael Mendez	Legendary Mexican trumpeter who emigrated to the United States. He was well known as a soloist, arranger, composer, and educator.
Tim Morrison	Soloist and former member of the Boston Symphony; soloist on major film recordings such as those for *Amistad* and *Saving Private Ryan*.
Sergei Nakariakov	Russian trumpet virtuoso born in 1977. He released his first CD at the age of 15. His recordings include works originally for violin, cello, and viola, many of them performed on flugelhorn.
Philip Jones Brass Ensemble	The numerous commissions of this ensemble, founded in 1951, helped catapult brass chamber music to a new level of virtuosity and visibility.
Anthony Plog	Soloist, educator, outstanding composer for brass instruments. Founding member of Summit Brass and Fine Arts Quintet.
Charles Schlueter	Soloist, recording artist, and Boston Symphony principal trumpet.
Gerard Schwarz	Recording artist; conductor of the Seattle Symphony.
Doc Severinsen	Leader and trumpeter for the *Tonight Show* band; Grammy award–winning trumpeter with more than 30 recorded albums, including big band, jazz fusion, and classical. Learned trumpet from a small instruction book with the help of his violinist father.
Susan Slaughter	Won principal trumpet with the Saint Louis Symphony Orchestra in 1972, making her the first woman to become principal trumpet in a major symphony orchestra.
Philip Smith	New York Philharmonic principal trumpeter; learned by spending time with the Salvation Army Band, where his father played cornet.
Marie Speziale	First woman trumpeter in a major symphony orchestra, playing for 32 years with the Cincinnati Symphony.
Edward Tarr	With more than 100 recordings to his name, Tarr is a foremost scholar and performer of Baroque trumpet and is known for publishing the complete edition of the trumpet works of the Italian Baroque composer Giuseppe Torelli. He was the first director of the Trumpet Museum in Bad Säckingen, Germany, from 1985 till 2004.

William Vacchiano	Trumpet professor at the distinguished Juilliard School for 67 years and principal trumpet of the New York Philharmonic for 38 years. His students include Miles Davis and Wynton Marsalis.
Allen Vizzutti	International soloist and trumpet pedagogue, visiting faculty at Eastman, and composer with works premiered by the Los Angeles, London, and Budapest symphonies.
Anton Weidinger	Invented the keyed trumpet; performed Haydn and Hummel on this instrument in the early 1800s.

Practice Sheet

Date of Lesson:

Warm-up:	
Long Tones:	
Lip Slurs:	
Intonation Studies:	
Major scales: Minor scales:	☐ Natural ☐ Harmonic ☐ Melodic
Lyrical etudes:	
Technical etudes:	
Articulations: Single: 　　　　　　 Double: 　　　　　　 Triple:	
Audition Material:	
Listening Assignment:	
NOTES from today's lesson/class:	

Beginning Practice Schedule

Use the schedule below, or work with your teacher to design a practice schedule that works for you, based on your needs and your teacher's requirements.

Warm-up   5 minutes

    Lip Buzzing

    Mouthpiece Buzzing

    Sirens

REST	2 minutes

Fundamentals

    Long Tones (Sound, Endurance, Muscle Memory)

    Tongued Articulations   15 minutes

    Slurs

    Rhythm Drills

REST	2 minutes

Repertoire

    Beginner Book Material

    Lesson Material (may overlap Fundamentals session   10 minutes
above)

REST	2 minutes

Warm-Down

    Long tones in the low register with little mouthpiece   3-5 Minutes
pressure

Listening

    Listen to great music and musicians   (Time as Needed)

Total: 35 minutes of playing, 8 minutes of rest

Intermediate Practice Schedule

Use this schedule as a starting point to design your own practice,
based on your available time and your goals as a player.

Warm-up

Lip Buzzing   10 minutes

Mouthpiece Buzzing

Long Tones

Rest	5 minutes

Fundamentals

Long Tones (Sound, Endurance, Breathing, Precision)   20-25 minutes

Tongued Articulations

Lip Slurs

Rhythm Drills

Intonation

Scales

Etudes (lyrical/technical)

Audition Music

Rest	15 minutes

Lesson Material

preparation for next week's lesson   20 minutes

material may duplicate the Fundamentals session

Rest	15 minutes

Band/Orchestra Music (time as needed)   10 minutes

Rest	5 minutes

Warm-Down

Long tones in the low register with little mouthpiece   5 minutes
pressure

Listening

Listen to great music and musicians   (Time as
                                                             Needed)

Total: 65 minutes of playing, 40 minutes of rest

Trumpet and Cornet Fingering Chart

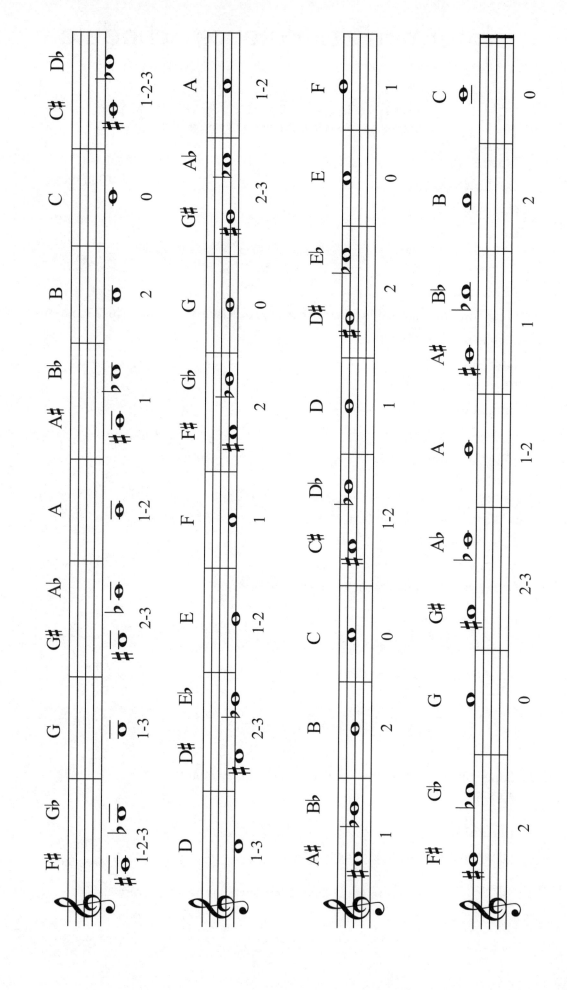

Mouthpiece Comparison Chart

The chart below provides a reference for equivalent mouthpiece sizes across various brands. The Bach system is often used as a standard reference simply because it has been around since 1918. This chart will help you know what your teacher or friends are referring to when they talk about a particular size.

This chart is for comparison only. Manufacturers give several measurements for their mouthpieces, including cup diameter, cup depth, rim width, and backbore diameter. The chart gives you a close comparison based on these dimensions, but there may be small variations in other dimensions—for example, while two rims may have the same diameter, one may have a more rounded, and the other a narrower, edge.

Your search for the perfect mouthpiece will continue as your playing evolves over time. This chart may help you more smoothly navigate those occasional transitions!

Bach	Yamaha	Schilke	Denis Wick	Monette
1C	TR 17C4	18, M1	1C, MM1.5C	B1-5
1 ¼ C	TR 17B4	17, M1.5	2W, MM2C	B2
1 ½ C	TR 16C4	16C4, M2	1.5C	B3
2C	TR 15C4	15C4	3, MM3C	
3C	TR 14B4	14	3C, MM4C	B6
5B	TR 14D4	13C4	4	
5C	TR 14C4	13	4B	
6C	TR 13B4	12	4B	
7C	TR 11C4	11	4B	B7F
10 ½ C	TR 8C4	9C4	5	B8

Transposition Chart

Music is written for …	B♭ Trumpet being played	C Trumpet being played	D Trumpet being played	E♭ Trumpet being played	A Piccolo trumpet played	Italian Tromba	German Trompete	French Trompet
Trumpet in C	M2 upward	as written	M2 downward	m3 downward	m3 upward, 8ba	Do	C	Ut
Trumpet in D	M3 upward	M2 upward	as written	m2 downward	P4 upward, 8ba	Re	D	Re
Trumpet in E♭	P4 upward	m3 upward	m2 upward	as written		Mi♭	Es	Mi♭
Trumpet in E	P4+ upward	M3 upward	M2 upward	m2 upward		Mi	E	Mi
Trumpet in F	P5 upward	P4 upward		M2 upward		Fa	F	Fa
Trumpet in G	M6 upward	P5 upward	P4 upward	M3 upward		Sol	G	Sol
Trumpet in A♭	M2 downward	M3 downward				La♭	As	La♭
Trumpet in A	m2 downward	m3 downward			as written	La	A	La
Trumpet in B♭	as written	M2 downward	M3 downward	P4 downward	m2 upward, 8ba	Si♭	B	Si♭
Trumpet in B	m2 upward	m2 downward				Si	H	Si

Names of Intervals

m2	minor second	P4	perfect fourth
M2	major second	P4+	augmented fourth, or tritone
m3	minor third	P5	perfect fifth
M3	major third	8ba	down one octave

Your music will state under the title of the work or on the left side of the page what trumpet key you are playing in. Use this chart to see what transposition you will have to use to play on the trumpet you have. A good transposition book will give you exercises to practice this essential skill.

Exercises and Technique Builders

Breath Control

Slow Breaths

Begin developing awareness of your breathing with long, slow breaths away from the instrument, using the correct embouchure.

1. Breathe in for 4 counts of one second, then breathe out for 16 counts.
2. Breathe in for 3 seconds, then out for 16.
3. Breathe in for 2 seconds, then out for 16.
4. Breathe in for 1 second, then out for 16.

As you decrease the number of counts, you will inhale the same amount of air in less time, without adding tension. Make sure your lungs can expand fully and you are not constricting the airflow.

Rapid Breaths

This exercise allows you to quickly fill your lungs with the desired amount of air. First, set your metronome at ♩ = 60. Form a correct embouchure, then perform the following steps at this tempo. Gradually increase your tempo 4–8 clicks at a time until you reach ♩ = 180.

1. Breathe in for 4 one-second beats, then breathe out for 16 beats.
2. Breathe in for 3 one-second counts, then breathe out for 16 counts.
3. Breathe in for 2 one-second counts, then breathe out for 16 counts.
4. Breathe in for 1 one-second count, then breathe out for 16 counts.

Dynamics

This exercise will train the respiratory muscles to work together. You may be surprised at the amount of control it takes to distribute your air equally! Form a correct embouchure, then:

1. Breathe in for two counts of one second each, then start blowing out slowly.
2. As you exhale, gradually increase the speed to its maximum, then reduce the speed. When you play, the result will be a smooth crescendo and diminuendo.
3. While doing this, keep the air flow as steady as possible. Make sure that you do not hear the air slow down, flutter, or quiver, keeping your chin steady.
4. Keep your lips in a constant position, maintaining a consistent opening without relaxing or tightening during the exhale.

Capacity

Without the instrument, exhale to your most empty point. Place your hands on your abdomen and continue to exhale. Feel the muscles in motion around the rib cage, supporting the air removal. You may be surprised how much air remains after you thought you had exhaled fully.

Now, with the instrument, inhale a shallow breath and play G for as long as possible while maintaining a good sound.

When you think you have run out of air, try to sustain the note for several more counts, without adding tension. You do not need to force the air out; simply keep breathing out.

Endurance

All of us would love to be able to run, practice, or perform without ever getting tired. As with any sport, playing trumpet is a physical skill that requires physical training in order to achieve strength, flexibility, and stamina.

Trumpeters, like athletes, can design a training program that enables them to achieve their performance goals.

When playing the trumpet, as opposed to sports, it is preferable to take a break when your embouchure muscles are physically tired. Don't try to be a hero. By resting often you are enabling your muscles to rebuild and recover without injury. During your pieces, take your mouthpiece off your lips as often as possible during rests, so that blood can return to oxygenate your embouchure muscles.

Playing in a relaxed way will also help you last longer. Unnecessary tension will cause all of your muscles to work harder, and muscles are strongest when they are relaxed and have adequate circulation.

Remember that poor air usage forces your embouchure to do more work than it needs to. Fast air allows your lips to resonate and vibrate more easily, taking the stress off your embouchure muscles.

Loosely flap your lips during rests, as though you were making a motorboat noise. This stimulates the muscles and increases circulation. Do not flap your lips too hard—a gentle lip flap is better and will also be less distracting to those around you.

Below are some exercises to help improve your endurance. Spread these exercises out over your weekly practice sessions, rather than going crazy and pushing yourself past your physical limit. A rule of thumb is to rest as much as you play.

Long Tones

Practice on long tones helps create muscle memory and strengthens the corners of the embouchure.

Long Tones with a Nose Breath

To build endurance, practice long tones as usual, but take a nose breath rather than breathing through the corners of your mouth. Keep the mouthpiece on your lips and do not relax the embouchure between notes. Rest when you are tired.

Etudes

Play Clarke *Technical Studies* #2 using good, supported, fast air. Gently tighten and relax your aperture to execute the exercise.

Lip Slurs

A lip slur refers to playing two notes in a row that use the same fingering. Lip slurs build endurance and control for your embouchure.

Lip Bends

Lip bend refers to changing the pitch of a single note without actually jumping to the next harmonic in the series. By keeping the corners of your mouth anchored while requiring the aperture to bend and flex, lip bends strengthen the corners of your mouth and build endurance.

If you approach your training like an athlete, you will be able to count on your physique to meet the demands of any performance situation.

Counting Beats

Below are examples of examples of counting subdivisions within various time signatures. When you get a new piece of music, count it out loud at first (without a metronome) until you are familiar with the pattern. Then add the metronome to establish strict time placement of the rhythms.

When tapping your foot, tap every beat and lift precisely on every eighth note. In measure two below, notice there will be two downward taps that don't coincide with a note change.

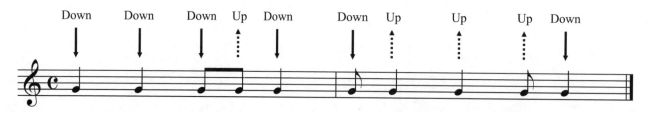

Metronome Practice Drills

Practicing music and exercises with a metronome needs to be part of your daily practice. It's tempting to skip metronome practice so you can get to your lesson or band material, but setting aside specific time to focus on your rhythm and tempo will raise your accuracy in other areas of your playing. It is almost always more efficient to practice one skill at a time! Over time you will spend less time working on the rhythmic figures in your music and have more time to work on the more musical aspects of your playing.

Practice these exercises beginning at sixty beats per minute and gradually increase the speed. Make sure the first note of each beat coincides exactly with the metronome click. Repeat each exercise as needed, and don't increase the speed until you can articulate each line clearly and accurately at the slower tempo.

Master each exercise before continuing down the page. Practice these short exercises daily, increasing your tempo and rhythmic accuracy gradually over many weeks and months.

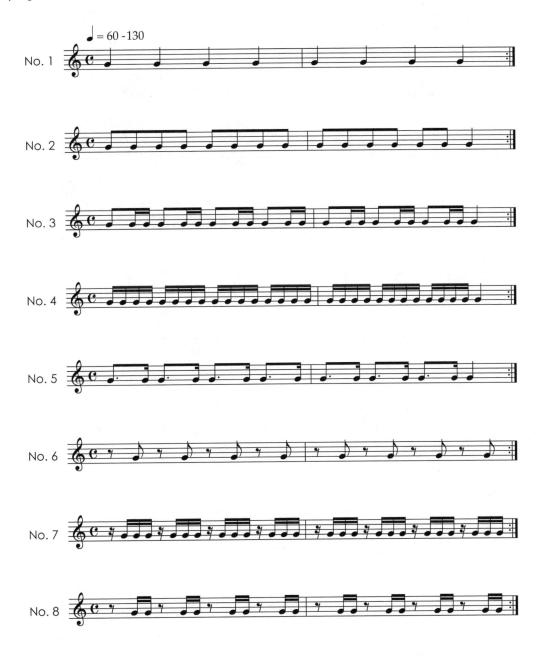

Ever-Expanding Buzz

Beginners: Play the exercise twice a week for 1–2 minutes sometime in the middle of your practice session. Increase to 5 minutes as you build endurance.

Intermediate players: Play the exercise three times per week, increasing the time gradually until you reach 10 minutes, or a maximum of 15 minutes.

Long Tones

Daily practice on long tones helps with range, power, endurance, and sound production.

Take a deep breath, making sure not to raise your shoulders as you breathe. Clearly articulate the note using "too," and hold for 8–12 counts. Breathe after each note, and begin the next note in the same way.

To increase the difficulty, play each successive note at a different dynamic level.

Exercise No. 1

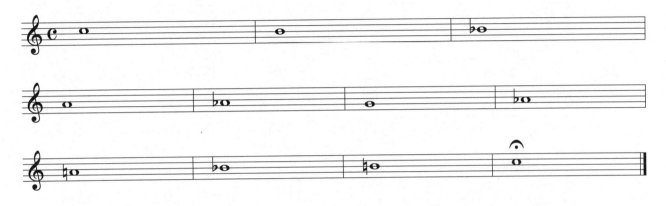

Exercise No. 2

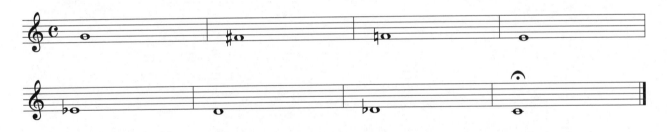

Exercise No. 3

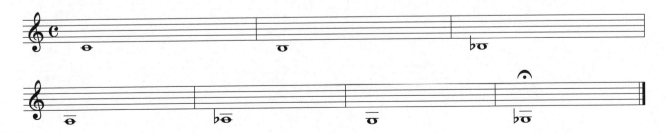

Extreme Dynamics

Practicing extreme dynamics will improve your sensitivity, confidence, and control in performance situations. Start each note as softly as possible. Gradually increase to fortissimo, then return to pianissimo. You will notice your aperture increasing with your volume. Check your intonation with a tuner as you crescendo and diminuendo, and keep your sound full and focused throughout. Each exercise follows the same dynamic pattern.

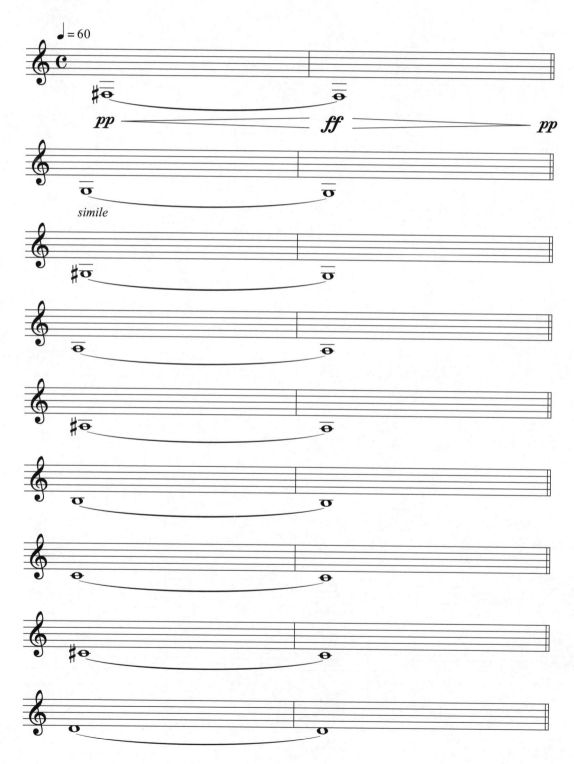

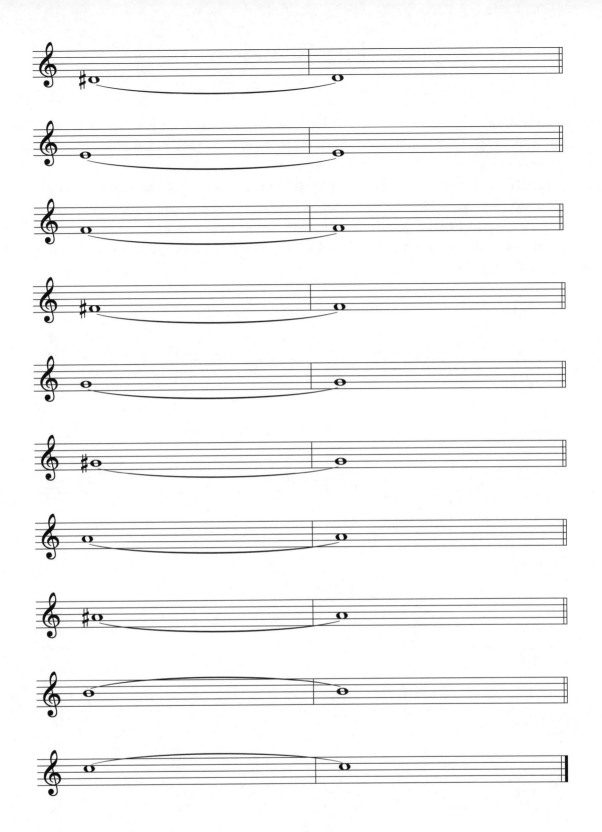

223

Lip Bends

Lip bends involve using the embouchure and tongue height to bend the pitch as far as possible—but without jumping up or down to the next overtone. In the exercises below, lower the pitch of each note by relaxing your embouchure and lowering your tongue.

Practicing this extreme "lip flexing" action will increase your strength, endurance, and lip flexibility. You will notice improvements in your high range, sound, ear training, and embouchure control.

Play each measure twice. The first time, use the valves to accomplish the pitch change; the second time, lip the notes down instead of using the valves. (Note: Pedal notes are fingered the same as they would be in the higher octave.)

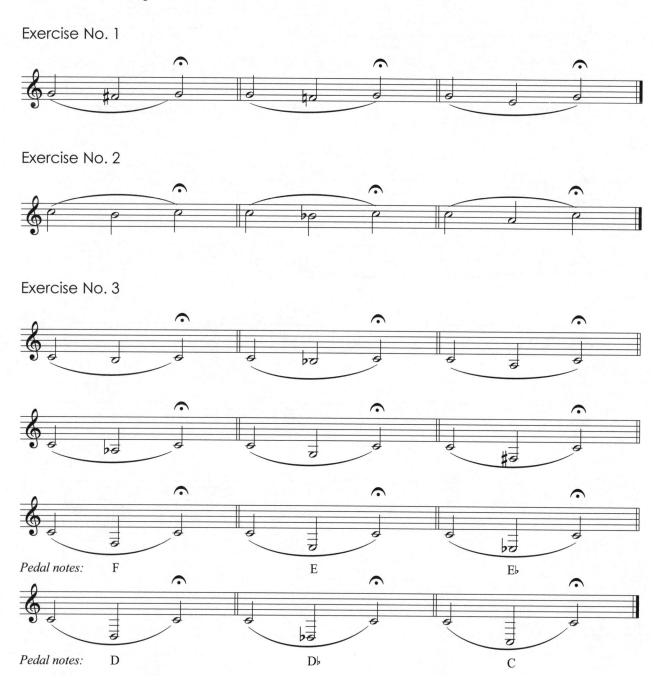

Lip Slurs

A lip slur is changing from one pitch to another within the same fingering, without articulation. To move to the higher note, tighten your embouchure and raise your tongue, keeping fast air at all times.

Start all the lip slurs slowly, then gradually increase the tempo for a trill effect. Keep the movement in the lips and the tongue; your jaw will move slightly as well. Be sure not to increase mouthpiece pressure for the higher note.

When slurring downward, loosen your embouchure and lower your tongue. Do not lessen the breath support; it may help increase your air slightly. Notice how the motions feel when you achieve the correct note, so you can repeat the same motions the next time.

Some larger intervals leap over a note in the harmonic series you're slurring within. If you're not careful, you'll hear the middle note as you jump between notes! To avoid hitting the middle note, imagine the sound of the pitch you want before you play it, and adjust your tongue and embouchure as quickly as possible.

225

No. 3

No. 4

Arpeggio Flexibility Study

This is a relaxing, beautifully lyrical exercise that will warm up your lips and sound for the day's playing.

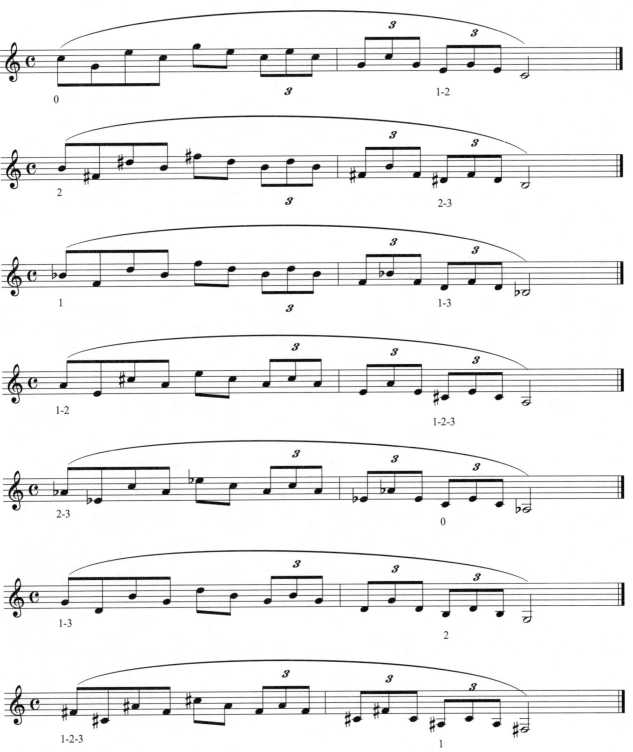

Eight On, Two Off

This exercise works well as an articulation or sound-development exercise.

Begin each line with a breath in tempo and play the line slowly, concentrating on your sound and articulation. Make the "too" or "koo" articulation as clear as possible while maintaining a full, rich sound. Play the notes either legato or separated, but be consistent from line to line.

Set your metronome initially to a slow tempo. Play precisely with the click, listening for accuracy, precise articulations, and sound quality. Increase the tempo gradually over time.

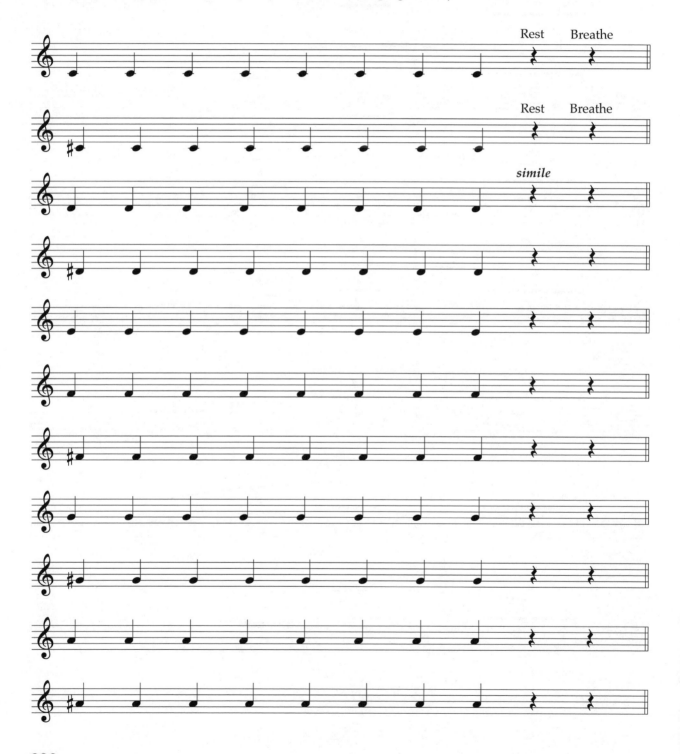

230

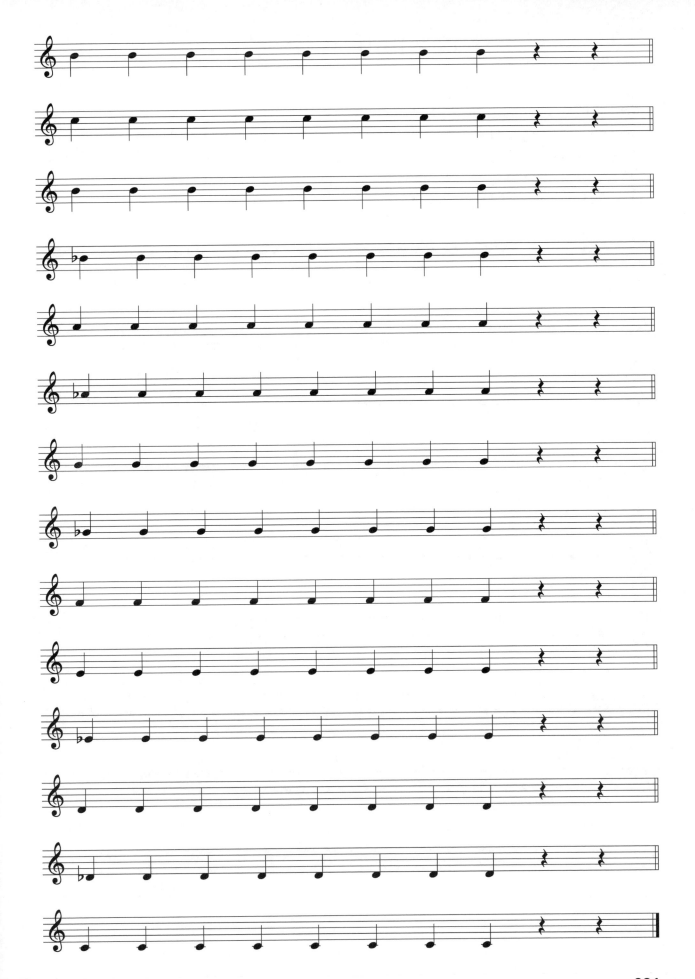

231

Articulation Studies

 Articulation Acceleration

This exercise is designed to develop the single "too" and "koo" articulation, both of which are required for a fast, accurate multiple-tongue. Clarity and consistency, not speed, are the most important goals of this exercise. Choose a speed that allows you to tongue clearly and accurately while keeping a steady beat. Increase your tempo gradually over many practices.

232

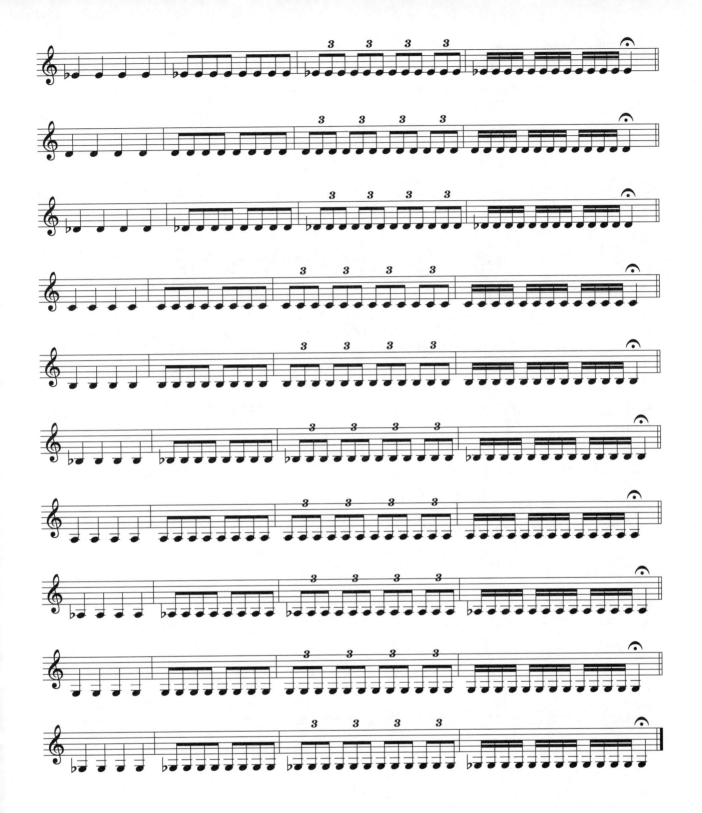

233

Articulate and Center

Establish a consistent, well-defined articulation on the "too" syllable. Breathe after each whole note, and listen for good intonation on each pitch. Accents are printed over each note to remind you to tongue slightly harder than usual for clarity and response. As you gain experience with the exercise, use a metronome and tuner to improve your intonation and rhythmic accuracy.

Articulation Challenge

Play this exercise with a steady sound, using no vibrato or musical shape. First play the exercise softly, then repeat the exercise at a loud dynamic. Maintain a round, even sound in both dynamic extremes.

More Articulation Drills

This exercise gives you an opportunity to achieve clear, accurate articulation in the lower register of the trumpet. Use fast air and keep your embouchure relaxed. You can use this exercise to practice whichever aspect of your tonguing needs the most work—single-tonguing "too," single-tonguing "koo," or double-tonguing.

Articulation Zigzag

Play this exercise with a "too" articulation, first in a loud dynamic, then in a soft dynamic. Alternate playing the quarter notes legato and staccato. Your goal is to maintain a steady sound and consistent articulation across the large intervals.

Legato Scales

This exercise is designed to develop a long, connected legato articulation. Tongue each note, but keep the air flowing for the full value of each note. Strive for a smooth, full sound.

Expanding Intervals

As the intervals increase, maintain an accurate articulation and listen carefully to your intonation. Use whichever articulation style you need the most practice on.

Articulation Descent

Practice in both staccato and legato, keeping a consistent "too" articulation. It is easy for the low notes to be less clearly defined; keep the pitches centered and your articulation consistent.

Marcato Drill

Play this drill using a heavily accented legato style, with only slight separations between notes. Strive for clarity, especially in the lower register. Use a fast air flow to provide forward direction through each measure.

Articulation Variations

Practicing your double- and triple-tonguing will also increase the speed of your single tongue. Remember that the double-tongue syllables are "too-koo," and triple-tongue syllables are "too-too-koo."

Practice multiple-tonguing slowly at first to develop clarity and accuracy. "Koo" will tend to be weaker than "too," so make sure this syllable speaks clearly. If your articulation isn't responding as it should, put the trumpet down and try just speaking the syllables; then practice with the mouthpiece alone.

The following melodies are simple compared to what you may be used to playing. However, their simplicity will allow you to focus on clean articulation, so that your other literature will sound even more brilliant!

Variation I

Variation II

Variation III

Theme

Variation I

239

Variation II

Theme

Variation I

Variation II

Variation III

No Split Notes

This exercise will increase your note accuracy by developing muscle memory for your embouchure and tongue positions. Keep your tempo slow, and use a metronome.

1. Start off with a breath in tempo: take a full half-note breath before you start each line.
2. Choose either the "too" or "koo" for each measure. You may change syllables between lines.
3. Take the mouthpiece away from the lips where indicated.

When you reset the mouthpiece after the rest, you are establishing muscle memory for your tongue height and embouchure.

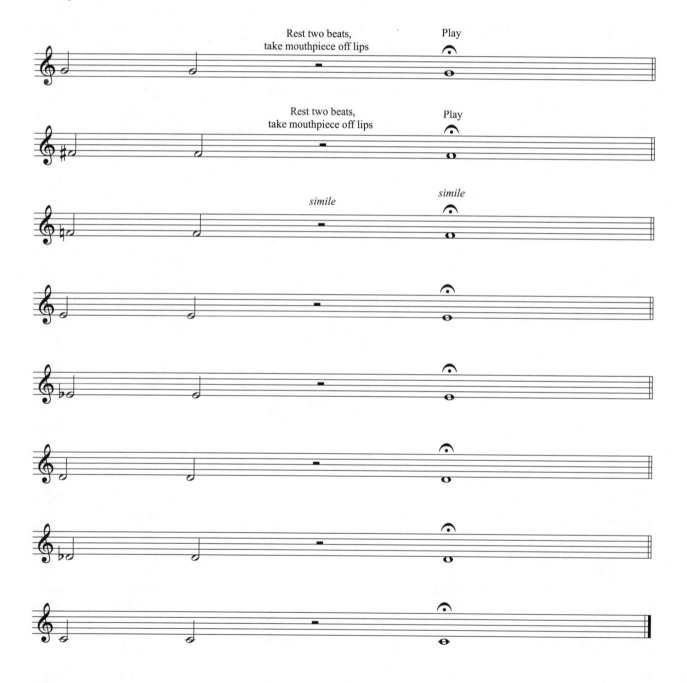

Accuracy Practice

Choose one articulation (staccato, marcato, or legato) and use it for the entire exercise, striving to make all of the notes identical in length, attack, and decay. Each note must have a full, centered tone.

Take a breath in time on beat four, and take the mouthpiece off the lips between notes.

Tongue and Finger Coordination

Good articulation requires that the tongue and fingers be coordinated. The tongue must strike at precisely the same time the valve is fully depressed or raised.

Finger each exercise silently, then play it on the trumpet. Listen for clarity and consistency in both the finger strokes and the articulation. Practice slowly at first, then gradually increase the tempo as your articulation and finger agility improve. Don't be afraid to slam the valves down while practicing this exercise—you can't hurt them! The goal is to develop excellent finger speed so that you have it when you need it.

Never lift your fingers off the valves while playing. This causes a longer stroke for your fingers and causes you to take more time to transition to the next note. In fast playing, every millisecond counts!

Exercise No. 1

Exercise No. 2

Exercise No. 3

Stamp's Warm-Up

While teaching at the University of Southern California in the heart of Los Angeles, James Stamp repeatedly found his students coming to lessons with their lips sore and swollen as they made money recording with movie studios. Some even experienced career-threatening injuries from the long hours and hard playing.

The exercise below is adapted from the warm-up and warm-down Stamp developed to prepare his students for these long hours of demanding playing. Perform these exercises on your mouthpiece at first, then play them on the trumpet. Your sound should be open, steady, and smooth. Make the phrase as connected as possible, and limit any sliding between the notes. The exercise should be played *non vibrato*.

For an excellent collection of studies to warm up various elements of your technique, purchase James Stamp's Book, *Warm-Ups & Studies*.

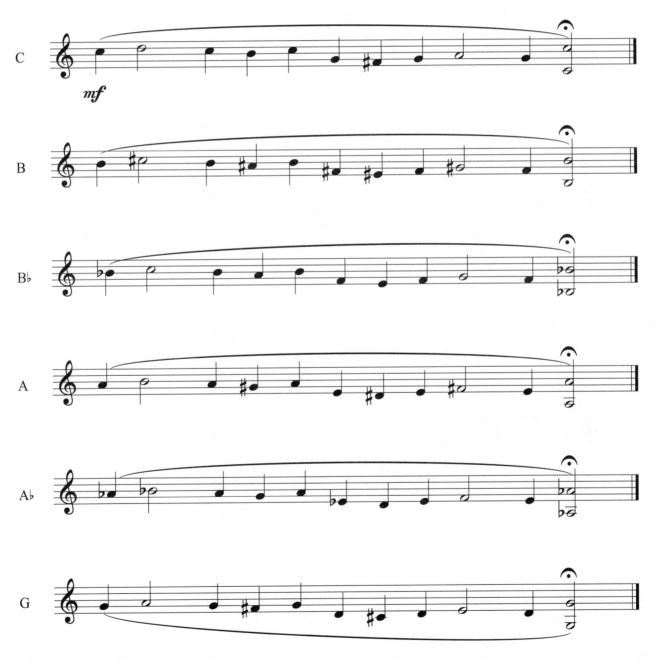

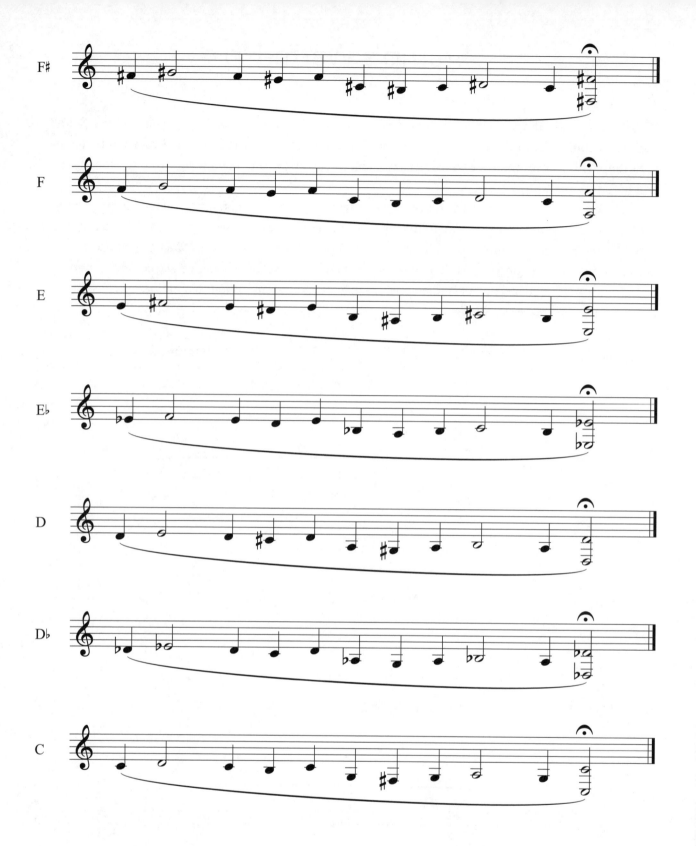

Developing High Range

Ascending Long Tones

Play each measure for 12 seconds. To work on embouchure strength, hold the embouchure and take a nose breath rather than breathing through the corners of your mouth. Play each exercise both loud and soft. Loud playing will develop the core of the sound, while the soft playing will develop embouchure strength and aperture and air control.

Lip Slurs

Use the indicated fingerings and lip slur between harmonics. You will tighten your embouchure and raise the tongue to move from lower to higher notes; relax your embouchure and lower your tongue to lower the pitch.

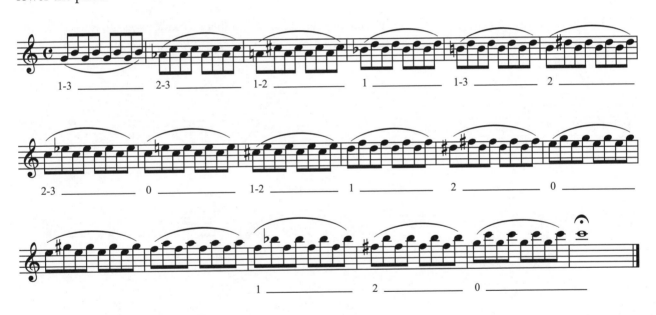

Arpeggios

Breathe only between measures, not within measures. As your speed increases you will be able to play more measures in one breath, ultimately playing the entire exercise in two breaths.

Harmonics

In the following exercise, play all of the harmonics between octaves (marked as glissandi). Some measures will have the same notes as in the previous exercise, "Arpeggios"; other measures will include additional harmonics.

Pedal Tones

Pedaling in Octaves

Pedal tones use the same fingerings as the corresponding upper octave. Keep your embouchure loose and relaxed, and your tongue in the "toh" position. Do not break the embouchure or pivot the instrument between the fourth note and the pedal note. Remember to use fast air! Strive to make the pedal notes as full and focused in sound as the higher-octave notes.

Descent into Pedal Range

Play the entire scale in two breaths, breathing where indicated. Practice both slurred and articulated, keeping your sound full and focused.

Finger Busters

These exercises make use of the third finger, an alternate fingering not typically found in your music. Practicing these unusual patterns will increase your coordination, dexterity and finger independence. Start each exercise slowly, and gradually increase the speed. The goal is to play the entire exercise in one breath.

Chromatic Exercises

Mixed Flats and Sharps

C Chromatic

High G down to Middle C-sharp

Middle C down to Middle F-sharp

Middle G down to Low C-sharp

Low C down to Low F-sharp

G Chromatic, 2 Octaves

C Chromatic, 2 Octaves

One-Octave
Scales

Scales on C

254

Scales on G

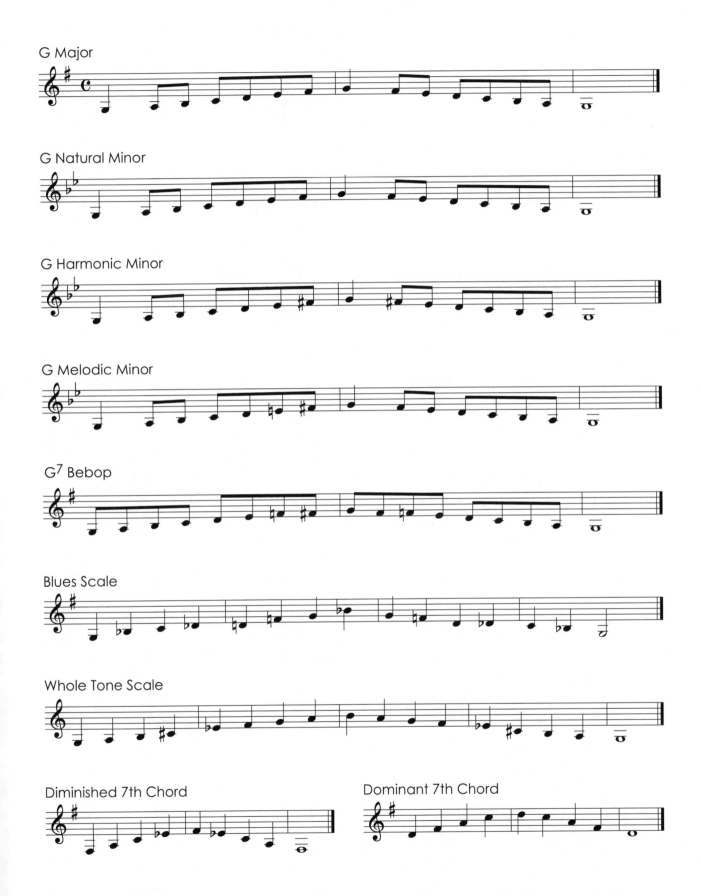

Scales on D

Scales on A

Scales on E

Scales on B

Scales on F♯

F♯ Major

F♯ Natural Minor

F♯ Harmonic Minor

F♯ Melodic Minor

F♯⁷ Bebop

Blues Scale

Whole Tone Scale

Diminished 7th Chord

Dominant 7th Chord

Scales on D♭/C♯

Scales on A♭/G♯

Scales on E♭

Scales on B♭

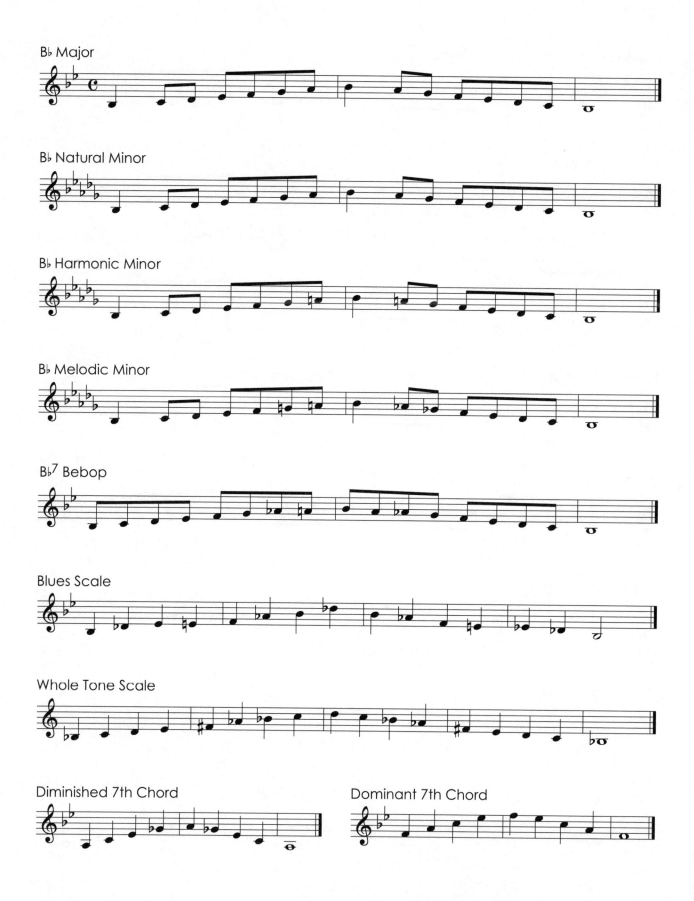

Scales on F

Two-Octave Scales

Scales on C

C Major

C Natural Minor

C Harmonic Minor

C Melodic Minor

C⁷ Bebop

Blues Scale

Whole Tone Scale

Diminished 7th Chord

Dominant 7th Chord

Scales on G

G Major

G Natural Minor

G Harmonic Minor

G Melodic Minor

G⁷ Bebop

Blues Scale

Whole Tone Scale

Diminished 7th Chord

Dominant 7th Chord

Scales on D

D Major

D Natural Minor

D Harmonic Minor

D Melodic Minor

D⁷ Bebop

Blues Scale

Whole Tone Scale

Diminished 7th Chord

Dominant 7th Chord

Scales on A

A Major

A Natural Minor

A Harmonic Minor

A Melodic Minor

A⁷ Bebop

Blues Scale

Whole Tone Scale

Diminished 7th Chord

Dominant 7th Chord

Scales on E

E Major

E Natural Minor

E Harmonic Minor

E Melodic Minor

E⁷ Bebop

Blues Scale

Whole Tone Scale

Diminished 7th Chord

Dominant 7th Chord

Scales on B

B Major

B Natural Minor

B Harmonic Minor

B Melodic Minor

B⁷ Bebop

Blues Scale

Whole Tone Scale

Diminished 7th Chord

Dominant 7th Chord

Scales on F♯

F♯ Major

F♯ Natural Minor

F♯ Harmonic Minor

F♯ Melodic Minor

F♯⁷ Bebop

Blues Scale

Whole Tone Scale

Diminished 7th Chord

Dominant 7th Chord

Scales on D♭/C♯

275

Scales on A♭/G♯

A♭ Major

G♯ Natural Minor

G♯ Harmonic Minor

G♯ Melodic Minor

A♭⁷ Bebop

Blues Scale

Whole Tone Scale

Diminished 7th Chord

Dominant 7th Chord

Scales on E♭

Scales on B♭

B♭ Major

B♭ Natural Minor

B♭ Harmonic Minor

B♭ Melodic Minor

B♭⁷ Bebop

Blues Scale

Whole Tone Scale

Diminished 7th Chord

Dominant 7th Chord

Scales on F

F Major

F Natural Minor

F Harmonic Minor

F Melodic Minor

F⁷ Bebop

Blues Scale

Whole Tone Scale

Diminished 7th Chord

Dominant 7th Chord

Index

A piccolo trumpet, 136
abdominal muscles, 62–63, 65
accuracy
    adjustment of, 109
    practice, 86, 243
acoustic, defined, 200
alternate breathing and buzzing, 64
alveolar ridge, 70, 100
anatomy
    breathing, 65, 66
    cheeks, 35, 98
    embouchure, 97, 98
    trunk of the body, diagram, 62
Andre, Maurice, 87, 205
angle
    bell, 21
    tongue, 100, 103
    trumpet, 20–23, 27, 175
anxiety in anticipation of performance,
    153–154, 159, 161
aperture
    explained, 31
    high notes, 121
    loud playing, 118
    low range, 110
    and mouthpiece, 138
    pedal tones, 124
    pencil hold, 105
    and pitch, 45, 73
    soft playing, 118
arms, head, and shoulders, placement, 20, 27
Armstrong, Louis, 205
arpeggios, 229, 248
articulation, 69–77, 230–241
    "breath attack," 77
    coordination, 72
    defined, 69, 200
    exercises, 230–241
    "goo," 77
    jaw movement, 72
    "koo," 71, 74–77, 230, 232–237
    "loo," 77
    note endings, 72
    "poo," 77
    single-tonguing, 71, 74, 232–233
    slurring, 73, 217, 225–228, 247
    speed, 72

"tee," 72, 100
    tongue strikes, 69–71
    "too," 69–71, 75–77, 230, 232–237
arts management careers, 188
asthma, side effect of beta blockers, 161
"at home" on stage, 162
attention, band jargon, 166
Aubier, Eric, 205
audiences. *See* performances and auditions
auralizing, use of imagination, 115
auxiliaries, band jargon, 166

bacteria growth in trumpet, 50
band
    careers, 188
    class, 86
    music stand posture and placement, 24
    See also marching band
Baroque period, 11, 200
baton twirlers, band jargon, 167
battery, band jargon, 166
Beethoven, Ludwig van, 142
beginning to play, 43–60
bell
    angle, 21, 23, 24
    construction, 126, 130
    depicted, 4, 5
    mutes, 127–129
    weight, 131
bellows, 63, 65
    See also breathing
bending pitch. *See* lip bends
beta blockers as anxiety-reducing drugs, 161
Blast, 205
blood circulation in lips, 50, 81–83
Bobo, Roger, 76
bore, 15, 58, 139, 200
    mouthpiece comparison chart, 213
braces on teeth, 141–145
    adjustment time after removal, 145
    cushioning, 142
    types of, 141, 142
bracing points, 57, 58
brass
    care for, 5
    repair, 183
    trumpet family, 132–136